LONGMAN BUILDING STUDIES

Hospital Architecture

LONGMAN BUILDING STUDIES

Hospital Architecture

**Paul James and
Tony Noakes**

Dedication:
To the designers, staff and patients
of the hospitals portrayed in this book.

Longman Group UK Ltd,
Longman House, Burnt Mill, Harlow,
Essex CM20 2JE, England
and associated Companies throughout the world.

© Longman Group UK Limited 1994

*The views expressed by Tony Noakes are not necessarily those
of the Department of Health or NHS Estates*

First published 1994

ISBN 0 582 09389 9

British Library Cataloguing in Publication Data
A catalogue record for this book is available from the British
Library

Library of Congress Cataloging-in-Publication Data
A catalogue record for this book is available from the Library
of Congress

Set by 3 in 8½/12pt Century Old Style
Produced by Longman Singapore Publishers (Pte) Ltd
Printed in Singapore

Contents

Key to drawings

Note on drawings

Acute general hospitals are large and complex buildings. They can contain up to 30 separate 'departments' each with different functional requirements. One large department may comprise over 100 small rooms. Space will not permit the inclusion of detailed floor plans. The drawings included under each example are intended to give a broad understanding of the concept. To help this process, departments of similar functional characteristics are grouped into three main 'zones' – nursing, clinical and support.

The key to hospital planning is the manipulation of these zones and their relationships to produce a fully functional integrated hospital. A diagram analysing the zoning strategy is shown at the beginning of most of the examples. Thereafter outline floor plans together with detail plans of some major departments are keyed to the following table listing the zones, departments and rooms.

The clinical zone

Accident and emergency
1   Resuscitation
2   Examination cubicles
3   Nurses' work space
4   Cleansing
5   Relative's overnight stay
6   Plaster suite

Administration and records
7   General office
8   Office
9   Records store
10   Diagnostic index
11   Shop

Day centre
12   Treatment/endoscopy
13   Day ward/space

Intensive therapy unit and coronary care
14   Multi-bed space
15   Single-bed room
16   Staff overnight stay
17   Equipment

Laboratory (service and teaching)
18   Haematology
19   Chemical pathology
20   Microbiology
21   Catheter lab
22   Histology
23   Blood bank
24   Specimen, reception, etc
25   Automated section

Mortuary
26   Body store
27   Viewing room
28   Post mortem

Teaching and training
29   Classroom
30   Seminar
31   Lecture theatre
32   Demonstration
33   Library

Operating theatres
34   Anaesthetic room
35   Exit bay/recovery
36   Scrub-up
37   Preparation
38   Disposal
39   Transfer, reception, bed park
40   Operating room/bay
41   Sterilising
42   Post-operation recovery

Out-patients
43   Consulting/examination rooms
44   Dental surgery
45   Snack bar/pantry
46   Sub-waiting
47   Dispensary

Obstetric delivery and premature baby
48   Delivery suite
49   Labour rooms
50   Cots and incubators

X-ray and radiotherapy
51   Radiodiagnostic room
52   Dark room/processing
53   Undressing cubicles
54   X-ray records/reception
55   Radiotherapy room
56   NMR

Preface

This book is one of a series which the publishers have commissioned on most major building types. Its format is similar to others in the series, in which an introductory chapter is followed by illustrated examples of recently completed buildings from many parts of the world.

The main purpose of the book is to inform architects, and others concerned with the design process, of current trends in hospital design. It is also addressed to hospital and health service managers and those who work in hospitals, in the hope that they will become aware of the potential for improvements of their working environment, and will entrust the design of future buildings to architects with the vision to achieve this potential.

This is a time of rapid change in medicine, in the organization of health care, in building and engineering techniques, and in architectural expression. We have approached the question of how designers may respond creatively to the problems which they are set, and how the users – the staff and patients of the hospitals – will benefit.

The introductory chapter does not purport to be a history of hospital building, although some examples from the past 30 years are referred to because of their influence on current work: neither is it a manual on how to design a hospital. There are many books in existence which have this aim. It does not go into detail on particular hospital functions and departments. In a number of countries, governmental, academic and other bodies have produced documents for this purpose, such as the Health Building Notes published by the UK Department of Health. Books and other technical publications of this sort are periodically updated as medical practice changes.

The intention of Chapter 1 is to present some of the factors that have influenced hospital design, and to point out those which, as the illustrated examples show, offer hope for the improvement of this building type.

Can hospitals be architecture?

The question 'can hospitals be architecture?' has often been posed. The answer may depend on how 'architecture' is defined. Pevsner began the introduction to *An Outline of European Architecture* with these words:

A bicycle shed is a building; Lincoln Cathedral is a piece of architecture. Nearly everything that encloses space on a scale sufficient for a human being to move in is a building; the term 'architecture' applies only to buildings designed with a view to aesthetic appeal.

It is, however, possible to argue that a well-designed bicycle shed can be 'architecture' and a dull and unimaginative cathedral merely a building. Is it architecture when the design was made with 'a view to aesthetic appeal', but when the resulting building was generally regarded to be a total failure in this respect? In other words, the description 'architecture' should be applied to the quality of outcome rather than of intention. This is more in accord with Henry Wotton's famous statement, based on Vitruvius, that 'In Architecture, as in all other operative arts, the end must direct the operation. The End is to build well. Well building has three conditions, Commodity, Firmness and Delight'. For Wotton, 'architecture' and 'building well', seem to be synonymous.

In this book, examples of hospitals, almost all completed since 1985 or, in a few cases still under construction, are illustrated and described. They are taken from many countries and as a result show the expected diversity due to different cultures and different functional requirements, but also some interesting convergences. They have all been selected as exhibiting, in our opinion, a good balance of firmness, commodity and delight: they use building and engineering technology effectively, they achieve their functional objectives, and are good-looking places to see and to work in. The functional and technical complexity of modern hospitals has often led to the neglect of aesthetic quality, thus raising doubts about whether they can, in either Pevsner's or Wotton's terms, qualify as architecture.

Both in countries where private hospitals are in competition with each other, and in those where a publicly funded health service has become increasingly aware of a need to make its patients feel more welcome, there has of late been greater emphasis on environmental quality. This has manifested itself in increased attention to landscaping, finishes and furnishings, and the use of works of art, either as permanent features, or as revolving exhibits. But, more fundamentally, it concerns total design of the building.

At a time of pluralism in architectural taste, the response of hospital clients and their architects has

◁◁ *London Bridge Hospital. View of atrium from first-floor corridor*

◁ *Sri Sathya Sai Institute of Higher Medical Science, Bangalore, South India.*

been varied. Hospitals have been less influenced by fashion than have office, domestic and retail buildings; although one or two examples show 'Post-Modern' influences, the majority are in the mainstream of modern architecture, with more emphasis on human rather than monumental scale, in spite of the large size of many of these buildings. There seems little likelihood of, or justification for, the application of traditional styles in this building type; the disparity between interior and exterior would be glaring.

The only apparent exception is in the revival, mainly in Arab countries, of Islamic architectural traditions: this may have the merit of fitness for climate, as well as cultural acceptability. It is also a tradition that is developing in response to the needs of new building types in these countries. The Indian example illustrated, Sathya Sai Institute of Higher Medicine p. 62, shows a similar influence of traditional Hindu architecture.

Architecture, change and obsolescence

It has long been axiomatic that the functional and technical success of hospitals depends on the ease with which they can grow and change, and that this dependence increases with time. The aesthetic implications of designing buildings whose ultimate extent and form cannot be predicted has received less attention. This is not a situation exclusive to hospitals; airports and universities face similar problems. An urban design approach is called for; an initial building whose form is geometrically finite will tend to look awkward when extended. The higher the buildings are, the greater the aesthetic as well as technical and functional difficulties of making a satisfactory addition.

These problems are compounded by the fact that many hospitals are built in several phases. This may be due to the successive replacement of old buildings on an existing site or limits to the amount of capital available at any one time, and to the capacity of the building industry to undertake very large contracts. A firmly established Development Control Plan is essential for a hospital built in phases – to lay down the strategic direction of later phases, but not, of course, of their detailed design.

The length of life for which hospitals are designed has a bearing on this. The case is made later for the 'long-life loose-fit low-energy' approach. There is, however, a point of view that grew up with the modern movement, of buildings as utilitarian and disposable objects – a case that has recently been

▽ St Thomas's Hospital, London, Henry Curry, 1867.
Plan in 1950 showing extensions in black.

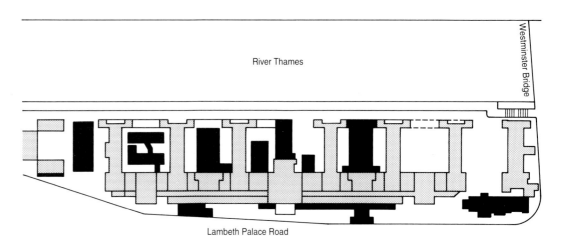

River Thames

Westminster Bridge

Lambeth Palace Road

argued intellectually by Cedric Price and Martin Pawley, and which is common practice in the USA, with its tradition of cheap timber-framed low-rise buildings. This thinking has also affected hospital buildings with potentially long-life structures, which tend to be replaced at an earlier age in the USA than in most other countries. An immediate cause has been structures which are too tightly tailored to the needs of initial users, and which become obsolete due to changing standards demanded by hospital accreditation authorities.

Adaptability may best be provided by a long-life structure, within which internal changes can easily be made. Ease of adapting existing engineering and drainage services, and of providing new services, is crucial to true flexibility. Departments or functions involving complex technology which are likely to grow can then be placed next to less demanding functions such as offices; the latter can be moved elsewhere when the former need to expand into their space.

The length of life debate has been highlighted by DOCOMOMO (the group concerned with the documentation and conservation of the architecture of the 'modern movement') in addition to the question of whether (and how) highly regarded works of modern architecture should be conserved and restored. It might be argued that the higher the aesthetic quality of hospital buildings, the greater the problems that later generations will have in radically altering or demolishing them when they become functionally obsolete. However, only the most cynical of clients would argue against high quality design on the grounds of ease of ultimate demolition.

An historical parallel in Britain is provided by the large Victorian psychiatric hospitals, many of them fine examples of 19th century design, and justly protected by listing as of 'architectural and historic interest'; alternative uses for them, however, are hard to find, and they frequently become the subject of disputes between conservationists and hard-pressed health authorities. The long-life loose-fit approach also has the virtue that when buildings are no longer suitable for hospital use, there is a

'Nucleus hospitals'

◁ *Maidstone, Powell, Moya and Partners, 1983.*

▽ *Bridgend, Alex Gordon Partnership, 1985.*

greater choice of alternative uses.

Wotton's description of architecture as an 'operative art' is significant: the longevity of buildings in not necessarily related to their architectural value. Whereas music and literature of inferior quality are soon forgotten, unattractive buildings can last as long as beautiful ones. This strengthens the case for setting high standards of architectural design in all health buildings. As a holistic approach to the needs and aspirations of patients becomes more widely accepted, the natural consequence is a demand for a high-quality environment, and one which will grow old gracefully.

3

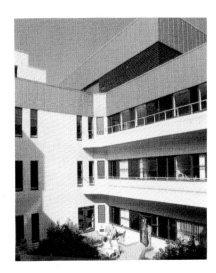

'Nucleus hospitals'

▷ *Croydon, Percy Thomas Partnership, 1982.*

▽ *Redhill, Hospital Design Partnership, 1982.*

The attributes that make for delight in building cannot be applied as a cosmetic afterthought. Good architecture is not achieved by advice or prescription, but only by the application of a high quality of imagination throughout the design process; this means the selection of a firm of architects whose work shows such quality, and, within a firm or public sector organization, an individual with this ability as lead designer. This applies as much to extensions and radical alterations to existing buildings as to new ones.

The British Nucleus hospitals are all similar in having standard departments accessed from a 'hospital street' or main circulation route. Nucleus is a planning and not a building system: there was a deliberate decision not to standardize the physical components of which they are composed. Many different firms of architects and engineers have produced their interpretation of these designs; some of the buildings are mundane and unimaginative, whereas others are very attractive. All have an overall similarity of form, and are built within the same cost limits. Sir Philip Powell (co-founder of Powell Moya Partnership, the architects of many hospitals, three of which use the Nucleus system) observed that one advantage of the Nucleus standardization is that 'it gives the architect more time to concentrate on the architecture'.

This may give the impression of the 'architecture' being applied as a cosmetic skin – the criticism that has been made of much recent commercial building. Experience of these hospitals shows, however, that the variations in aesthetic quality are more than skin-deep, and are found equally in the handling of spaces, and in interior design.

An excuse often offered for the disappointing architectural quality of hospitals is that so much time and attention has to be given to the details of functional design and the complex mechanical and electrical services associated with them, that too little time remains for aesthetic considerations. Their technical complexity may discourage many imaginative architects from tackling these problems; they may also be disinclined to take on a building type with relatively little scope for sculptural or spatial effects and, although entrances, atria and dining rooms give some scope for exciting three-dimensional treatment, it has to be admitted that hospitals are mainly assemblages of fairly small spaces. Nevertheless, as the examples in this book show, there is scope for architects to bring pleasure to experiences which are inherently anxious or painful for patients, and to the working life of dedicated staff carrying out difficult and stressful tasks.

Hospital location, context and urban design

In the age before widespread car ownership, hospitals were usually located in or near the centre of towns. Only asylums for the mentally handicapped or ill, and sanitoria and fever hospitals were located out of town, partly to effect isolation, partly because of cheap land. As suburbs developed, some new hospitals were established, but patients still tended to travel to the old town-centre hospitals, which often had the prestige associated with a medical teaching role. Eventually, these sites became too crowded for further expansion, and some were forced to move out.

In towns which only needed one major hospital, a move to the edge of town was a solution that became more practical as more staff, patients and visitors travelled to hospital by car. Emergency access could be easier, as greater distances tended to be offset by avoidance of town centre traffic congestion. Accident and emergency departments found a reduction in their load of 'casual' attendances; presumably those with minor conditions went to their general practitioner or a pharmacist instead – a more appropriate solution to their problems.

However, the out-of-town hospital is controversial, for ecological reasons, as leading to more car travel, and on social grounds. The draft local plan of an English city included a policy statement that 'the Council will oppose the closure of general hospital facilities in the city, unless alternative provision is equally accessible by city residents, and especially those without access to a car'. This was in a city with 46% of households without cars, and a far larger proportion of the population without use of a car at any one time. These are also the older and poorer people with greater health service needs. Good bus services may make the greenfield edge-of-town location acceptable, but there are growing pressures to move away from this approach. Centrally located hospitals can reduce site congestion by off-siting support functions; all hospitals can solve access and ecological problems by increased collaboration with primary care services, for example, by hospital specialists holding clinics in health centres and general medical practice buildings, and by introducing information technology links to them. This is dealt with in Martin Valins' companion volume *Primary Health Care Centres*.

The architectural character of the hospital should be influenced by its surroundings. The greenfield site imposes fewer restraints, mainly those of fitting well into the landscape; this can be enhanced by earth moulding and early tree planting. Wexham Park is a striking example of an architect's response to landscape; the original plan, with a slab block of wards above a podium, was abandoned, and a mainly single-storey design substituted, because of its architect's reaction to a fine established landscaped park, and his wish that patients should have as close a contact with it as possible. The extent to which use of local materials is desirable depends on their continued and economic availability, and on whether there is a strong local architectural character.

In a city the problems are much greater, depending on the image which the hospital wishes to present. In the USA, the ward towers of the Hill-Burton hospitals of the 1950s and 1960s dominate low-rise residential suburbs. A more friendly and less strident image is now preferred; this calls for respect for the scale as well as materials of neighbouring buildings. A striking historical example is provided by the original Victorian pavilions of St Thomas's Hospital, London, which exchanged a happy dialogue with the Houses of Parliament across the Thames, a dialogue rudely interrupted by the white-tiled towers of the 1970s.

The greatest challenge to the architect is to build a large new hospital on a small urban site. The Chelsea and Westminster Hospital, London, is a recent example. It is, of course, much easier to present a relaxed, informal and friendly image on a large site, as hospitals such as the West Dorset Hospital, Dorchester, (p. 130) and Conquest Hospital, Hastings (p. 124) show.

The image of the hospital

The 12th annual Thomas Cubitt Trust Lecture was given in London on 26 September 1990 by Lord Gowrie, a former Minister for the Arts in the UK Government. Entitled 'Architecture and the Ruined Millionaire: A Plea for Anarchy', it dealt largely with the way we look at buildings – both as works of art and as useful objects – and the effect they have on us. Lord Gowrie commented that 'In Britain, our grandest, in the sense of largest, buildings over the past 20 or 30 years have been offices of administration and hospitals'. He observed of two London hospitals that 'St Thomas's white-tiled clinicism faces Barry and Pugin's (and perhaps London's) masterpiece: The Houses of Parliament. Further down the Thames from St Thomas's is Guy's Hospital, which is my candidate for the ugliest building in London. A cross between an up-ended industrial spanner and some awful building out of Kafka – Guy's profile wrecks Tower Bridge from everywhere but the South – I am sure that Guy's is a great hospital with dedicated staff. But, if you had to enter it, wouldn't your morale sink even lower?' He then quoted from Philip Larkin's 1972 poem, 'The Building', (published in *High Windows*, reproduced with the permission of Faber & Faber).

▷ Guy's Hospital, London, Watkins Gray International (p. 70).

The Building

Higher than the handsomest hotel
The lucent comb shows up for miles, but see,
All round it close-ribbed streets rise and fall
Like a great sigh out of the last century.
The porters are scruffy; what keep drawing up
At the entrance are not taxis; and in the hall
As well as creepers hangs a frightening smell.

There are paperbacks, and tea at so much a cup,
Like an airport lounge, but those who tamely sit
On rows of steel chairs turning the ripped mags
Haven't come far. More like a local bus,
These outdoor clothes and half-filled shopping bags
And faces restless and resigned, although
Every few minutes comes a kind of nurse

To fetch someone away: the rest refit
Cups back to saucers, cough, or glance below
Seats for dropped gloves or cards. Humans, caught
On ground curiously neutral, homes and names
Suddenly in abeyance; some are young,
Some old, but most in that vague age that claims
The end of choice, the last of hope; and all

Here to confess that something has gone wrong.
It must be error of a serious sort,
For see how many floors it needs, how tall
It's grown by now, and how much money goes
In trying to correct it. See the time,
Half-past eleven on a working day,
And these picked out of it; see, as they climb

To their appointed levels, how their eyes
Go to each other, guessing, on the way
Someone's wheeled past, in washed-to-rags ward clothes.
They see him too, they're quiet. To realise
This new thing held in common makes them quiet,
For past these doors are rooms, and rooms past those,
And more rooms yet, each one further off

And harder to return from; and who knows
Which he will see, and when? For the moment, wait,
Look down at the yard. Outside seems old enough:
Red brick, lagged pipes, and someone walking by it
Out to the car park, free. Then, past the gate,
Traffic; a locked church; short terraced streets
Where kids chalk games, and girls with hair-dos fetch

Their separates from the cleaners – O world
Your loves, your chances, are beyond the stretch
Of any hand from here! And so, unreal,
A touching dream to which we all are lulled
But wake from separately. In it, conceits
And self-protecting innocence congeal
To carry life, collapsing only when

Called to these corridors (for now once more
The nurse beckons –). Each gets up and goes
At last. Some will be out by lunch, or four;
Others, not knowing it, have come to join
The unseen congregations whose white rows
Lie set apart above – women, men;
Old, young; crude facets of the only coin

This place accepts. All know they are going to die.
Not yet, perhaps not here, but in the end,
And somewhere like this. This is what it means,
This clean-sliced cliff; a struggle to transcend
The thought of dying, for unless its powers
Outbuild cathedrals nothing contravenes
The coming dark, though crowds each evening try

With wasteful, weak, propitiatory flowers.

Philip Larkin
(9 February 1972)

Readers who did not know that Philip Larkin spent much of his career as Librarian of Hull University might still have recognized 'The Building' in this poem as the main building, completed in 1968, of Hull Royal Infirmary. It typifies much that has proved unpopular in the buildings of its period: a

△ 'This clean sliced
cliff...', Hull Royal
Infirmary, UK, YRM,
1969.

person approaching the sheer 15-storey cliff-face
of its front elevation is dwarfed to insignificance.
The scale of the building arrogantly dominates but
totally disregards the mainly two-storey buildings
of the surrounding 19th century streets. There is
no relief in the endless repetition of vertical and
horizontal elements of the design; there is, of
course, no 'immoral' ornament; although the
disastrous error of exposing concrete in northern
climates was avoided, it is clad in uniform grey
mosaic, and there is thus no chromatic or textural
relief.

The main entrance and waiting area has a run-
down airport lounge appearance; the accident and
emergency department and the first floor out-
patient department are now being upgraded, but
the deep plan form of the four-storey podium leads
inevitably to long corridors without natural

lighting, and far too many internal working spaces.
Only when the upper floors containing wards are
reached is any compensating advantage found, in
the extensive views over the flat Humberside
landscape.

This criticism of a typical hospital of a recent
generation is not made for the sake of knocking
down an already fallen idol, but rather as an
instance of what later designers have reacted
against. The move away from very tall buildings is
explained later, on mainly technical and functional
grounds.

Flat roofs are inextricably associated with tower
and podium designs. It is an irony that Le
Corbusier's argument for flat roofs was to permit a
greater freedom of plan-form, but the rigid
geometry of Miesian buildings does not avail itself
of this freedom. The flat roofs of the 1960s stem

8

from the rectilinear obsession of the mainstream modern architecture of that time.

It is perfectly possible (even in Britain, whose winters contain so many freezes and thaws that put severe stresses on integral roof finishes) to design a flat roof that insulates and keeps out the rain. But it is not cheap or simple, and still requires careful maintenance. Le Corbusier and his followers allowed themselves some sculptural freedom in engineering and other roofing structures, for example at the Unités d'Habitation and in the Golden Lane housing in London. In the hands of less skilled architects, the clutter of rooftop shapes, especially in highly serviced buildings like hospitals, can be chaotic and ugly. The enclosure of these elements within a pitched roof protects both the engineering plant, and maintenance staff servicing them; the only special consideration needed is access panels for the removal and replacement of plant. In less highly serviced areas, there may be the possibility, either initially or by subsequent attic conversion, of providing offices and other less specialized accommodation within the roof space.

The psychological message of the pitched roof is of shelter from rain and other elements and is a compelling one in all but very dry climates. Many of the hospitals illustrated in this book have probably adopted pitched roofs both as a logical covering for blocks of mainly similar width, and for their emotional appeal.

In Cuzco, Peru, a flat-roofed office block built in the historic Inca and Spanish city led to public protest and the requirement of red-pantiled pitched roofs for new buildings, including the new hospital. As the illustrations show (p. 89ff), these have been built, and, in addition, a very interesting elevational treatment has been achieved. It provides the variety and contrast that was lacking in the phase of Modernism which was obsessed with endless repetition of uniform elevational elements. The projecting windows of the wards on the top floor cling to the overhanging eaves. The 'interstitial' sub-floor for engineering services has small openings for light and ventilation, thus

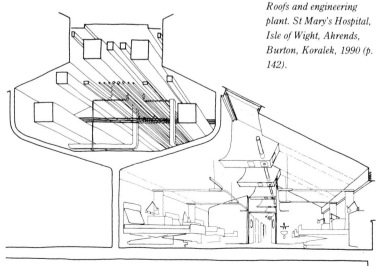

Roofs and engineering plant. St Mary's Hospital, Isle of Wight, Ahrends, Burton, Koralek, 1990 (p. 142).

solving the problem of a greater than usual floor-to-floor height better than most of the interstitial hospitals since Greenwich. The two lower floors have windows appropriate to the diagnostic and service functions. The great length of the elevations is broken up effectively by vertical shafts. A similar differentiation between fenestration of different floors is apparent in St Mary's Hospital, Isle of Wight (p. 142ff) and Lambeth Community Care Centre, London (p. 154ff).

The Low Energy Hospital Research Study recommended roof lighting to wards, which in the Isle of Wight are thus mainly at top-floor level; the need for windows on these floors is therefore reduced. At Lambeth the hole-in-the-wall

▽ Cuzco Hospital, Peru, 1986, Cooper, Grana, Nicolini (p. 88).

fenestration of the ground floor contrasts with the larger windows in the ward floor above, with french windows onto the roof terraces.

Traditional ornament has depended largely on craft skills, especially in wood and stone carving. These skills are no longer readily available, but one of the forms of enrichment that has been revived in recent years is that of decorative brickwork, where the use of more than one colour or texture of brick, and of arch or corbel forms add interest in a way that can grow logically from the nature of the material and the construction. This has been well used at Lambeth, with the additional enhancement provided by the Della Robbia medallions. The main entrance and gable ends are marked by modern versions of classical pediments,

features which in other forms are used in Edmonton and Utrecht, but which stop short of arbitrary facadism.

These are some of the ways in which recent hospitals, like buildings of other types, have sought to enlarge the language of architecture. In a few cases, there may be a tendency towards that form of Post-Modernism that finds fun in applying elements of classical or other historical styles, but usually only produces an unnatural and ludicrous effect, as with a moustache on the Mona Lisa. But it is hoped that the examples as a whole illustrate a healthy form of pluralism – an artistic exploration of means and ends, in order to produce delight for the beholder.

Imagination has been similarly applied to interiors such as the high-level colour-banding used by Powell, Moya and Partners first at Maidstone, then at Hastings, and developed further in the Great Ormond Street Children's Hospital. At Lambeth, a virtue has been made of necessity, in the green stained wood battens covering electrical services, as, in the interests of economy, there are no false ceilings.

The use of atria has proved very successful in producing lively and attractive spaces – notably at Chelsea and Westminster (where they also contain the main circulation route), at Edmonton and at the London Bridge Hospital.

Vertical or horizontal hospitals

The past 20 years have seen a steady move away from hospitals organized primarily around vertical circulation systems. This trend has been most marked in the UK, where the Nightingale-inspired horizontal pavilion hospital never died out, as it did in many other countries. It persisted between the World Wars, and was revived in the mid 1950s in the Vale of Leven Hospital in Scotland. In another form, it reappeared in Wexham Park Hospital at Slough, designed by Powell & Moya (with John Weeks) in the late 1950s. This was a seminal building; its village form led in one direction to

Weeks's Northwick Park Hospital, and, in the other, by the development of its wide-span structural design, to the Greenwich Hospital. The low-cost two-storey hospitals at Crewe and Airedale designed by Paul James were also influenced by Wexham Park, both in the ward plans and in the overall layout. Paul James and Howard Goodman, the architect of Greenwich, collaborated to produce the 'Best Buy' hospitals (designed 1967 and completed 1973 and 1974 at Bury St Edmunds and Frimley) in which the influence of their earlier schemes was brought together. This in turn led to Nucleus hospitals, which are mainly of two or three-storey construction, comprising standard departments on either sides of a hospital street, a zone combining main circulation and services distribution.

Developments in some other countries have been influenced by British ideas – for example, that of Greenwich on the USA Veterans Administration System, and particularly its prototypical hospital at Loma Linda in California. The same logic that drove the British sequence of developments has been evident in other countries. The problem of vertical organization, and particularly a tower block of wards, is that of a limited envelope with no means of lateral expansion. The considerable proportion of each floor taken up by lifts, stairs and service shafts is not only inherently wasteful and expensive, it also makes the plan form more rigid, and inhibits subsequent alteration. Growth of a vertically-organized hospital tends to take the form of clusters of smaller blocks at its base, with increasingly difficult service and circulation routes. Tall buildings are more likely to need expensive climate control, to consume more energy, and have greater problems of evacuation in cases of fire than have lower ones, in which horizontal evacuation is through successive protected zones further away from the source of the fire.

The advantage frequently claimed for tall hospitals is that they occupy less land. This is only generally valid for those inner urban hospitals, such as the (moderately) tall Chelsea and Westminster Hospital, London, (p. 68ff) where the floor area is

11

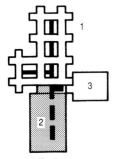

1. Nursing zone
2. Clinical zone
3. Support zone

▷ *Airedale Hospital,*
Yorkshire, UK, 1969,
Booth, Hancock, Johnson.

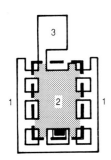

1. Nursing zone
2. Clinical zone
3. Support zone

▷ *'Best Buy' Hospital,*
Frimley, UK, 1972,
Hospital Design
Partnership.

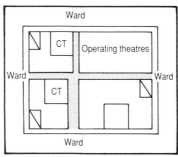

△ *Typical 'tower on podium' hospital. District hospital, Brig, Switzerland (I + B Architekten).*

◁ *Greenwich Hospital, UK, 1969, DHSS Hospital Design Unit.*

similar at all levels. The commonest type of tall hospital, especially in the USA, is the 'tower on podium' form, popularized by Gordon Friesen with his mineworkers' hospitals, and based on a production engineering principle of supplies fed to the wards from a basement service centre. The podium of these hospitals usually spreads to occupy a site similar to those of compact low-rise hospitals. The flexibility limitations of such hospitals becomes more evident as the proportion of the total built volume comprising wards is tending to diminish.

The tower and podium form is common in other building types, notably – and for similar reasons – hotels. Lever House in New York had a great influence, and not only on other office buildings. Although the earliest Friesen hospitals pre-date Lever House, the prevalence of hospitals of this form in the USA from the 1950s onwards may be partly attributable to a much admired 'classic' of modern architecture.

It is arguable, however, that hospitals, with their functional complexity and unknown ultimate form, are more suitable for the alternate organic stream of modern architecture, typified by Wright, Aalto and Scharoun, than for the purist geometry typical of Mies and his followers. It may be significant that Aalto's Paimio sanatorium is the only hospital among the undisputed masterpieces of modern architecture.

Structure and bays; windows and universal space

In the 1960s, two seminal British hospital designs, at Northwick Park and Greenwich, developed in parallel. In both, growth and change were regarded as prime criteria; much has been written about the contrasting development control plans that emerged on these two sites. Less has been said about the different approaches in these hospitals to structure and space planning.

There was much debate in the 1960s about the ideal structural bay width, which was generally taken to be between 6.30 and 7.20 m (21 and 23 ft). The main determinants were the width of a multi-bed room, and of a laboratory – the latter taken to be half of the former. At Northwick Park 7.20 m (22'8") was chosen, and a servicing strategy of vertical ducts associated with structural columns was adopted. A similar approach was used by YRM in a number of projects, such as St Thomas's Hospital, phase 2.

At Greenwich, however, the structural columns were placed outside the external envelope, a wide 19.50 m (64') span was chosen, and services were provided from the 'interstitial' spaces or service sub-floors between each floor of the hospital. The intention was to provide a 'Universal Hospital Space' that could be used for a wide range of different functions in the lifetime of the hospital – and good use has already been made of this flexibility.

These contrasting ways of handling structure and space planning may be observed in the examples illustrated in this book. They also have a considerable effect on the relation of windows to structure, and thus on the external appearance of the buildings – as long, that is, as the structure is expressed externally at all. The elevational treatment of Northwick and Greenwich presents a curious paradox. At the former, the policy of housing each main function or group of functions in a separate block led to some of these, and particularly the wards, having identical window patterns on each floor; but the spacing of the external structural mullions is related to the load supported, thus they are further apart on upper floors. This visual indeterminacy is probably deliberately symbolic of the indeterminacy principle fundamental to the planning of this hospital. The mullions at Northwick are placed so as not to encroach on usable floor space – a technique taken further at Greenwich.

Curiously, although the different blocks at Northwick are of different height, bulk and function, they all (apart from the glazed hospital street) have a similar appearance. Wexham Park expressed the 'village' idea better, by different forms of

14

construction and expression of the different parts of the hospital.

At Greenwich, however, each floor is planned without reference to those above or below, and thus the fenestration varies from floor to floor. However, the visual strength of the structural frame makes these variations in mullions secondary, and indeed quite hard to spot.

These two approaches to structure and space still persist. The Nucleus hospitals, in direct line of descent from Greenwich, share its concept of 'Universal Hospital Space' – indeed, each cruciform template is identical in shape for a number of different functions, and each can be placed above or below any other one. The position of internal columns is not related to specific functional dimensions; a column-free 16 m (52′5″) span is possible, but, for cost reasons, has only been used

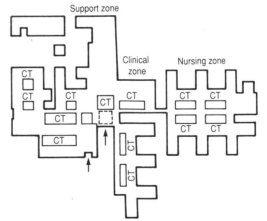

Support zone

Clinical zone

Nursing zone

△ *Wexham Park Hospital, Slough, UK, 1966, Powell, Moya and Partners.*

◁ *Plan.*

on the upper floors in some schemes, notably at Maidstone and the Isle of Wight.

The economics of column spacing are influenced by soil conditions; where deep foundations are needed, there is an advantage in reducing their number. Long-span beams present problems of vibration and deflection, which must be designed for; the benefit is greater freedom of planning, both initially, and, more importantly, when making later alterations. Most Nucleus hospitals have resolved the visual problem of variations of fenestration by emphasizing the horizontality inherent in these buildings: elevations thus comprise strongly marked bands, with solid spandrel bands separating window zones which have either glazing or solid panels as needed.

To reduce heat loss, window areas have been steadily reduced from those in the hospitals of the 1960s where continuous wall-to-wall glazing was usually the norm. These had the advantage of flexibility, provided that mullions were close enough together (0.86 m, 2′10″ at Northwick) or that their positions could be changed (on a 0.60 m, 2′0″ planning grid, at Greenwich). Recent designs which provide bands of interchangeable windows and solid panels have an advantage over those where

windows are openings in an external brick wall; research is warranted as to whether hospitals avail themselves of opportunities to alter external glazing, and to what extent 'hole-in-the-wall' fenestration inhibits flexibility.

Exposed concrete was common as an external material in the 1960s. Experience of its weathering problems has led most recent British hospitals either to return to brick cladding or to use metal panel systems. (Even in the clean air of the high Andes, the concrete external walls of the Cuzco hospital were painted.) These choices of materials, together with the pitched roofs that are now most frequently used, both for ease of maintenance and to provide a convenient and enclosed location for engineering plant, are producing a generation of hospitals with a horizontal emphasis which are more human in scale, more welcoming and more likely to exist in harmony with neighbouring buildings and the landscape. The distinctive character that has resulted is similar to that which in other building types (such as many of the schools in Hampshire, England), has been labelled in the UK as 'romantic pragmatism'.

Deep planning was the norm in the podium of tower and podium hospitals, and in other very

▽ Nucleus systems – universal hospital space in standard cruciform templates.

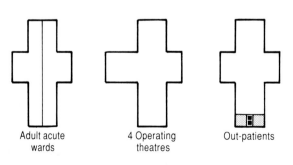

Adult acute wards

4 Operating theatres

Out-patients

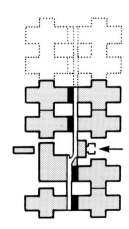

compact buildings such as Greenwich. In climates where the whole hospital has to be air-conditioned, this may be justified, but the psychological ill-effects on staff working in windowless rooms for long periods are well established; this applies particularly in high stress areas such as intensive therapy units. Natural lighting is desirable to all but stores, sanitary and other ancillary rooms, and natural ventilation can also be provided in blocks of up to about 16 m (52′5″) width; this allows for mixtures of rooms of different sizes.

Narrower block widths have the advantage that even ancillary rooms can have windows; they can thus later become offices, or other rooms that need daylight, a gain in flexibility that has been experienced in the West Dorset Hospital. This arose because of changes in the specialties for which some wards were used. (There is evidence that the recent NHS reforms in the UK may increase the incidence of such changes of use.)

Logistics, circulation and service systems

Hospitals have been likened to small towns. They contain residential areas, offices, workshops, laboratories and, most significantly, main circulation routes often described as hospital streets. The way in which these parts are assembled, as a coherent whole but with the parts differentiated, make for analogies with urban design; the way in which traffic moves, and the routes that are taken by mechanical and electrical services are fundamental generators of the plan.

The trend to lower-rise construction has not in all cases altered a mainly vertical pattern of traffic and movement, as in the case of two unbuilt designs of the 1960s, which typify the functionally stratified hospital – Le Corbusier's design for Venice, and the model hospital of Clibbon and Sachs. Both place their beds on the top floor, an arrangement with the potential for a pleasant naturally-lit environment. The Venice design would, however, have provided a uniquely awful and inhuman environment for care – indirect roof lighting with no view and semi-cubicles in which patients could not see each other or communicate adequately but could (unless the inter-communicating doors were amazingly

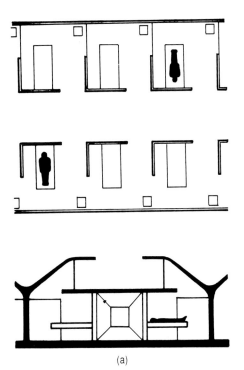

(a)

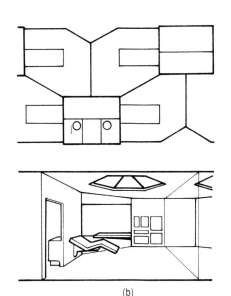

(b)

◁◁ *Plan and cross section of Le Corbusier's Venice hospital project, 1964.*

◁ *Plan and section of 'patient station', Clibbon and Sachs, 1969.*

17

soundproof) hear much that happened to and around their fellow patients. Clibbon and Sachs proposed out-patient and diagnostic and treatment functions at ground-floor level, and service functions at an intermediate level.

Similar in concept is the Cuzco design (p. 89ff) which more conventionally places service functions at the lowest level, using the slope of the site to give access to it and the floor above it. The latter consists of out-patient and diagnostic and treatment departments; the engineering services required are contained in an interstitial service floor. Above this, the red-roofed wards are placed around courtyards, in the manner of Spanish houses.

The main planning innovation at Greenwich was to minimize vertical transportation by siting (for example) all surgical beds, operating theatres and the intensive therapy unit on the same floor. This approach has been followed in the Best Buy and Nucleus hospitals and, among the hospitals illustrated in this book, those at Homerton, West Dorset, Hastings, Scottsdale, Oman and Abu Dhabi. Single-storey hospitals, such as Wexham Park, have, of course, the advantage of related departments all being accessible on the same level. Travel distance becomes the limitation; Wexham Park, designed as a 300-bed hospital, is probably

near the practical limit for a single-storey design. Avoidance of dependence on lifts is particularly important in countries where maintenance and availability of spare parts are unreliable; long waits for lifts are a major cause of inefficiency and of frustration to hospital users – they are more likely to be a problem in tall buildings than those of relatively low rise.

Greenwich was also the first hospital to have 'interstitial' spaces or service sub-floors between each hospital floor. This plan is most strongly justified in hospitals where the climate makes air-conditioning – or at least mechanical ventilation – necessary throughout. The enlarged space for trunking, pipes and wiring means a greater overall building volume, but the ability to reach and service them without entering the working areas above or below is an advantage; full benefit is only reaped if three-dimensional zoning for all the services is established. The best result has been achieved in the system developed by George Agron of Stone, Marraccini, Patterson (SMP) and Ezra Ehrenkrantz for the Veterans' Administration Hospitals in the USA, as shown in the Houston VA Hospital. SMP, together with contractors for some of the VA hospitals, have become convinced that hospitals with interstitial spaces throughout can be built at no

▷ *Cross section of Greenwich Hospital, UK. Completed 1969. DHSS Hospital Design Unit.*

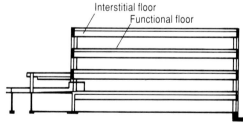

Interstitial floor
Functional floor

greater cost than hospitals with conventional demountable ceilings. This is largely due to the possibility that different trades can work simultaneously in the interstitial spaces and working floors, plus the increased speed of construction that can result. There is considerable scope for economy in maintenance and subsequent alteration to services.

Another Greenwich innovation was the use of escalators to all four levels. This removed the frustration of waiting for lifts, especially at peak hours for movement of staff and visitors. It is, of course, suitable only for a compact building of fairly low rise.

The movement of supplies has been also facilitated by the provision of ramps. Used in the Greater Baltimore Medical Center (1966) and then in the Best Buy and some of the Nucleus hospitals, construction time and use of cranes have been saved when the ramps have been built early and used by the contractor for movement of materials. The use of tug and trolley systems for distribution of linen and other supplies, and other topics relating to hospital logistics, are dealt with at length in *Hospitals: Design and Development* by Paul James and William Tatton-Brown.

The process of designing and building hospitals

In the initial planning stage, the most crucial decision is the purpose of the hospital. From this its content can be derived. Options for its provision must then be appraised: will it be located on one or more sites? Can existing buildings be retained and converted? (This implies that their condition and potential have been assessed.) What are the capital and (in the long term more importantly) running costs? What are the benefits? Proper analysis at this stage can avert fundamental and irreversible mistakes.

In *Primary Health Care Centres* by Martin Valins, the process of briefing is dealt with in depth. The smaller size of these buildings means that the designer is generally briefed by the eventual users, which is much less likely to be the case in hospitals, but the principles he states are generally valid – that the designers and representatives of the users must come to understand each other's language, and that the process is an iterative one. In other words, the designer's first sketch interpretations of the brief may throw the brief into question; both may be modified until it is agreed that the design

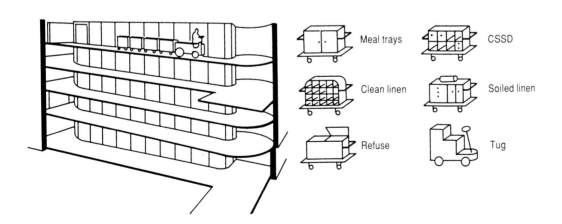

Meal trays

CSSD

Clean linen

Soiled linen

Refuse

Tug

◁ *Spiral ramp, locomotive supplies train and train components, Greater Baltimore Medical Center, USA.*

19

provides what the users will need. The 'Design Briefing System' is a check-list and aid to recording decisions; it and the 'Activity Data System' for identifying activities and their space, equipment and engineering service requirements are two aids to the briefing and design process that have been developed for the UK National Health Service, and are closely associated with the 'Health Building Notes'.

The development of standardization, whether of construction details, or of plan forms such as Nucleus, has the advantages that more research can be warranted than for a one-off design, and feedback from evaluation can lead to improvements in subsequent projects. There is, however, the risk of a mindless bureaucratic approach leading to the continued use of a design which is already out-of-date, or that is inappropriate to the proposed use.

The complexities of the briefing, design and construction process are such that in Britain a project manager is generally identified, with the ultimate responsibility for ensuring that the project is completed to the client's satisfaction within the intended time and cost targets. Increasingly, the project manager has the responsibility for appointing architects and other consultants. Fee competition for consultants is generally required. This has been widely criticized: firms may be tempted to submit too low a tender, and then have to carry out the design in a perfunctory manner, or to claim extras for any work not clearly specified in their terms of engagement.

In the traditional design process, the architect is the leader of the design team, and contractors tender for the work of construction. In an alternative approach, 'design and build', the contractor has total responsibility for design and construction, so that the client has only one party to deal with. The risk is that the architect's first loyalty will be to the contractor, with his need to make a profit out of the project. If there is a real partnership between architect and contractor, a satisfactory result may be achieved. The West Fife Hospital, (p. 148ff) was the result of a design-and-build competition; its success results partly from

the thorough brief prepared by the client health authority.

These variations on the design process have resulted partly from criticisms of the excessive time which it has often taken in the past. Reasons have included long debates on the content or location of the hospitals, and of the details of brief or design. Late changes in design – worst of all when these occur during construction – often cause increases in cost as well as delays. A design and briefing system, and standard designs can reduce the time-span, if used appropriately. Delays and extended planning periods have been criticized by governments, but a major cause of delays is a shortfall of public funding; all too often, designs are held up for a year or more and there is then the dilemma of whether the design should be updated, leading to further delays, or alternatively the design is taken down from the shelf and the risk of increased obsolescence accepted. This risk can be mitigated by omitting from the contract areas subject to doubt, such as X-ray rooms for which selection of equipment is best left as late as possible. These will then be the subject of separate contracts late in (or after) the main contract period.

The operational policies on which the brief is based should become the basis of operational manuals for the users. During the commissioning period, when equipment is installed, and staff are recruited and trained, these manuals should enable the users to understand the reasons for the form of the building. They should reduce the complaints that are often encountered during the early stages of the use of a new building.

When the building has been in use for about a year, design-in-use evaluation should be undertaken. This may be a low-key affair if intended mainly to test the adequacy of the design, and identify any post-contract changes needed. A more thorough evaluation may be warranted if it is to be used as guidance for the planners of subsequent projects.

Health services and their hospitals

The content and nature of hospitals is dependent on the kind of health services within which they function. For example, most British hospitals have an extensive out-patient department, in which most consultations with specialists take place; it is only general practitioners whose offices or 'surgeries' are in smaller buildings in the community. In the USA, where fewer physicians are described as general practitioners, and many patients go direct to the specialist relevant to their condition, 'medical arts buildings' have flourished, containing not only many consulting suites, but also radiological and laboratory facilities. These may be built close to the hospitals to which their physicians admit their patients, and in consequence those hospitals may not include out-patient departments as such.

The hospitals included in this book illustrate the wide range of buildings so defined, from a small community hospital to large and highly complex medical teaching centres. Almost the only thing they have in common is the provision of beds for in-patient care. 'Day hospitals' which patients, usually elderly or psychiatric, attend during the day and return home at night, are only included where they form a part of a hospital with beds, in which case the day hospital is usually located close to in-patient and out-patient accommodation serving the same specialties. These day hospitals are used mainly for patients attending regularly over a period of weeks or months, for rehabilitation services such as physiotherapy, occupational therapy and speech therapy, and ongoing medical and nursing care.

A different form of day care exists for individual medical or surgical procedures for which the patient can be prepared, treated, and recover either in the course of a morning, afternoon , or a whole day. New anaesthetic agents and new surgical and endoscopic techniques mean that 50% or more of all surgical operations can be done on a day basis, even allowing for the fact that to be suitable for such treatment, patients must be in good general health, have transport home, and someone to look after them there.

Day surgery units in the USA are often, like 'medical arts buildings', off the hospital site and may be simple short-life buildings, although the operating theatres need to be designed to the full standards (for example of air-conditioning) of those in the main hospital. Leaders of The British Association of Day Surgery favour self-contained units with their own or dedicated theatres, preferably with direct access and assigned car parking. Some authorities advocate free-standing units close to hospitals. Land for such units may not be available, and the site problem is compounded by the need to plan for expansion, since throughput may double or triple in the future. In some UK hospitals, day surgery units have been provided by building or converting wards close to existing operating theatres. Proximity is important to ensure good control over all the phases of day surgical care, and to minimize movement of patients.

In addition to operating theatres, rooms for endoscopy and lithotripsy may be included in a day surgery unit; its day ward may be used for day patients undergoing tests or medical procedures.

This subject has been dealt with in greater length than other comparable matters because it is one which will have a great impact on most hospitals in the coming decade. A hundred years ago, wards (or in-patient accommodation) accounted for well over half of the space in any hospital. In many modern hospitals, they may constitute as little as a quarter, and this proportion may reduce further.

The form of the ward or nursing unit has, however, a great influence on the shape of the building blocks or elements comprising the hospital. Key issues are the number of beds in each room, and the number in the ward, or area under the charge of a sister or head nurse. The American preference for all single rooms, and the British norm of 70–85% of beds in four, five or six-bed rooms, with the remainder in singles, lead to very different plan forms and ones which cannot easily be converted one into the other. They are influenced by cultural and economic factors, changes in which need to be predicted as far as possible. In order to achieve compactness of planning, some American hospitals have adopted a circular or, increasingly – as shown in two of the illustrated examples – a triangular plan form. The more specialized the form of the ward, the greater the difficulty of accommodating other functions above or below. If a conscious decision is taken to plan like above like, this is not a problem initially, although subsequent adaptability may be compromised. The extent to which the same building envelope can contain different functions has been tested by the Nucleus programme, and in some individual hospitals, such as McMaster Health Science Center, Hamilton, Ontario, Canada. These examples show that a shape such as the Nucleus cruciform template can accommodate some departments more satisfactorily than others; however, the greater the interchangeability, the greater the probability of long-term adaptability.

Facilities management

Many hospitals, and other large buildings, now appoint a facilities manager, with responsibility for housekeeping services (such as linen, catering, security and porterage) as well as estate and energy management. The facilities manager is also likely to have the role of planning and briefing for changes of use and modification to the building fabric.

With one exception, the hospitals included in this book are new buildings. Their adaptability will be tested by time; their long-term success will also depend on the skill of those responsible for their maintenance and modification to serve changing needs. There is scope for a further book on the practical yet creative adaptation of existing hospital buildings.

Just as in the design of a new building, the briefing of the designers by the users or their representatives is crucial: the immediate needs of the users must be satisfied, but not in a manner so rigidly tailor-made that any change of practice will be obstructed. Artistic skills are also required if alterations are to make an attractive upgrading which still respects the architectural character of the original building.

Hospitals, (and in centrally-organized health services, health authorities), have responsibilities for the efficient use of considerable resources of land and buildings. Skills in estate or facilities management are required if the best use of these resources is to be made. This calls for analysis of the condition of the building fabric, engineering services, energy efficiency, safety (fire etc.), and of their suitability for their function as well as whether they are being used to their full capacity. If the assessment of the hospital's holdings of land and buildings is carried out in parallel with, or in response to, a rationalization or rethinking of its service intentions and business plan, then there will be the best chance of a good fit between the buildings and the functions that they house.

Estate utilization studies in the UK have shown how fuller and more effective use can be made of existing buildings, and have influenced the nature and location of new buildings. Energy efficiency includes not only energy-conscious design of new buildings, and improved insulation, heat recovery and other aspects of existing ones, but also the management and development of a hospital estate that is energy efficient in wider aspects – for example, in minimizing use of cars by patients and staff. Telemonitoring of patients, and electronic links between GP surgeries and hospitals offer great scope for saving traffic and costs, as well as adding to the convenience of the patients.

Facilities management will also involve the disposal of superfluous land and buildings. This may involve analysis of alternative non-health service uses, where economics or conservation as historic buildings indicate retention. Avoiding unnecessary demolition saves energy on account of the energy consumed in construction and in the manufacture of building materials. There is also the possibility of buildings being used partly as hospitals and partly for other purposes. The need for flexibility may well in the future lead to multi-purpose structures.

Selection criteria for examples illustrated

The examples illustrated and described in the following chapters have been selected as being some of the more forward-looking designs from many parts of the world. In addition to the 'firmness, commodity and delight' criteria already mentioned, it was the intention to present a wide range of sizes and types of buildings that have been completed in the past few years, or which are still under construction.

Examples from 'third world' countries have generally been excluded: in the past, there have been far too many cases of Western-style medicine, with buildings to match, being imposed inappropriately. (The Sathya Sai Institute of Higher Medicine hospital in India (p. 64ff) is an exception; planned for an international body, it is by intention a world resource.) Due partly to the influence of the World Health Organisation, the role of primary care and basic health workers has been emphasized. Social, climatic and infrastructure factors make all health buildings in these countries, including the hospitals, a subject worthy of a separate study.

No examples of separate psychiatric, mental handicap, or geriatric hospitals are included. Mental handicap (otherwise known as mental retardation or learning difficulties) is generally seen as requiring social and educational rather than medical provision. In this field, as with mental illness, 'care in the community' – living where possible in normal housing, with day centres and other support systems – is now recommended. Some of the hospitals illustrated include acute psychiatric or geriatric units, serving day-patients as well as in-patients. For longer-stay accommodation, both for mentally ill and for elderly people, the trend in many countries is for provision in the community in hostels or nursing homes, and ideas of care and treatment are changing rapidly. Nursing homes are included in *Caring Environments for Frail Elderly People* by Geoffrey Salmon.

In attempting a world-wide coverage, the authors are all too aware of the difficulty in spotting the most recent and innovative schemes, and it is certain that, by the time of publication, there will be further new hospitals which we should like to have included. In a subject so influenced by indeterminacy as the design of hospitals, it is inevitable that any book on the subject must perforce be indeterminate.

CHAPTER 2

**International
examples 1980–90**

Specialist/Teaching Hospitals

David Grant Medical Center, Travis Air Force
Base, Fairfield, California, USA

Veterans' Administration Medical Center, Houston,
Texas, USA

Mackenzie Health Sciences Center, Edmonton,
Alberta, Canada

University Teaching Hospital, Essen, Germany

University Teaching Hospital, Utrecht, The
Netherlands

Central Emergency Hospital, Abu Dhabi UAE

Sri Sathya Sai Institute of Higher Medical Science,
India

Chelsea and Westminster, UK

The Hospital for Sick Children, Great Ormond
Street, UK

Guy's Hospital, UK

David Grant Medical Center, Travis Air Force
Base, Fairfield, California

Architects:	**NBBJ Group, Seattle**
Type:	**armed services hospital for USAF personnel and dependents, 375 beds (575 beds in emergency situation)**
Gross floor area:	**75,188 m^2**
Area per bed:	**200 m^2**
Site:	**55 acres within Travis base campus; parking for 1400 cars**
Delivery timescale:	**planning and design 22 months construction 1985–88 (Oct.) opened December 1988 total period five years**

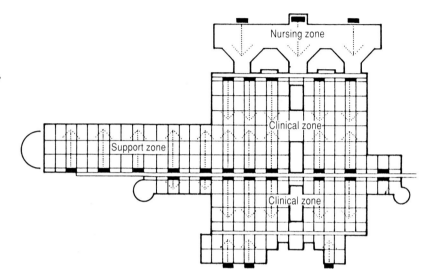

△ *Schematic plan showing relationship of zones*

Planning and design summary

Development concept
horizontal zones united by primary spine corridor and service duct system; interstitial service floors; four storeys maximum

Functional content

Specialties:	general medicine – 68 beds
	general surgical – 68 beds
	paediatric – 21 beds
	aeromedical – 75 beds
	obstetric/gynaecology – 28 beds
	intensive care and coronary care unit – 28 beds
	psychiatry and drug dependency – 52 beds
Clinical services:	accident and emergency operating theatres – eight suites diagnostic X-ray and scanning – 14 rooms radiotherapy nuclear medicine cardiac investigation out-patient clinics laboratory

Named after a World War II pioneer of aeromedical evaluation, the David Grant Medical Center is planned to ensure military readiness in the event of war. In addition it provides comprehensive medical care for 750,000 airmen and their dependents drawn from eight states in the Pacific region.

The large flat site is within the California earthquake zone; soil conditions are poor, and there is a high water table that prohibits basements for service areas and car parking. Instead the extensive parking lots are screened by landscaped berms which enable access to the four-storey hospital at two main levels.

Admissions and visitors are routed to the main entrance on the lower level. Out-patients and day-patients enter from the upper level forecourt. All supplies are received at the lower level well away from the patient entrances.

A central north/south concourse connects the two patient entrances and links in to the main east/west spine corridor system which incorporates the lift shafts and vertical service ducts leading to the upper levels. The structural columns and ducts are also co-ordinated with these corridors so that each functional zone has uninterrupted space for flexible internal layout.

25

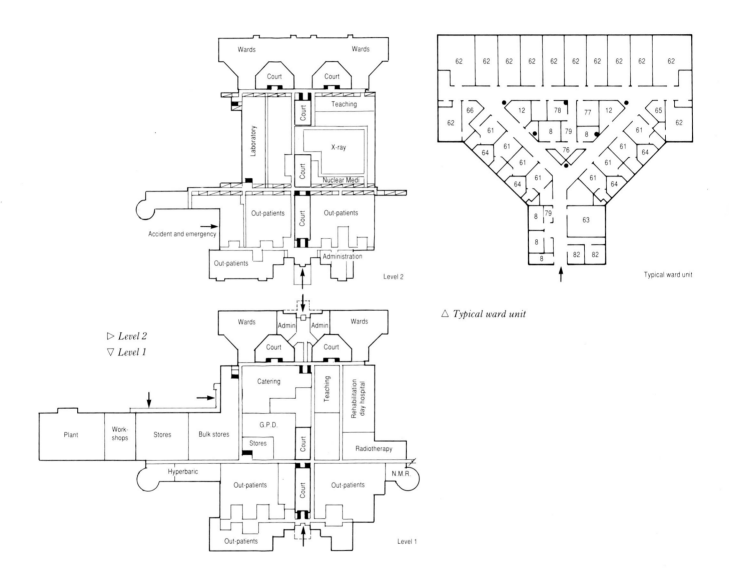

▷ *Level 2*
▽ *Level 1*

△ *Typical ward unit*

△ *General view of hospital showing two-level access*

The corridors are open-ended to permit future extensions along the east/west axis.

The planning of the nursing units follows the triangular pattern now well established in recent acute hospitals in the USA (see Veterans' Administration Medical Center p. 31ff). Beds arranged in single or double rooms, each with en suite bathrooms, require much longer access corridors than do multi-bed wards with common toilets.

Circular, square or triangular plans reduce the apparent length of corridors and can cut down on the movement of patients and staff.

The staff base and supporting utility rooms are placed centrally. From here the entrance to the unit can be controlled and all patient rooms are a short walk away.

All patients can enjoy natural light and external views. However, staff when not with patients, work in windowless rooms.

The bedrooms are sized and serviced to accommodate more beds in an emergency.

The building system integrates a steel frame and truss system with modular roof top plant components that feed all mechanical and electrical services vertically through dedicated shafts and horizontally through interstitial floors to individual departments. It is claimed that the use of these sub-floors will permit remodelling internally as well as vertical and horizontal expansion at minimum cost without interfering with ongoing hospital functions. There is no doubt that this 'systems approach' did contribute to a very fast construction schedule. A large and complex building was planned, designed and built in a total of five years, a remarkable achievement when compared with average delivery times elsewhere of 10–15 years.

The external finish is stucco painted in polychromatic bands which, together with the few windows and external service towers, give an appearance of great strength, rather like a massive desert fortress.

△ *View of typical two-bed room*

▽ *Schematic section showing mechanical distribution*

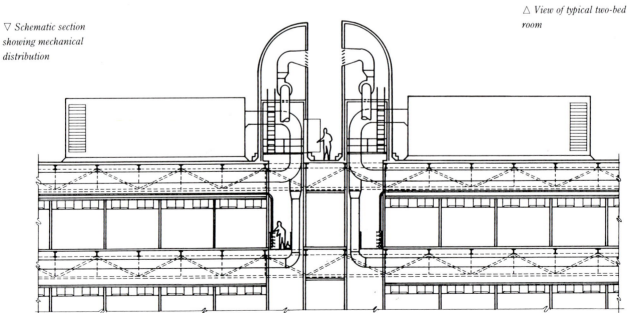

▷ *Staff restaurant*

▽ *Aerial view of hospital*

Veterans' Administration Medical Center, Houston, Texas

Architects:	**Stone Marraccini Patterson, San Francisco**
Type:	**acute general hospital for ex-servicemen and their families, 1044 beds**
Gross floor area:	**140,000 m²**
Area per bed:	**132 m²**
Site:	**large site in suburban Houston**
Delivery timescale:	**planning, design and construction 1983–90**

Planning and design summary

Development concept
universal space – interstitial building system design developed by architects for a number of VA hospitals throughout the USA

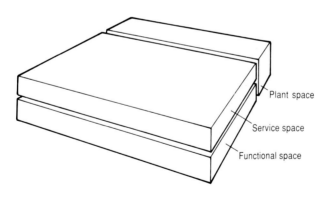

Plant space

Service space

Functional space

Functional content

Specialties:	general medicine
	general surgical
	neurology
	cardiology
	intensive therapy
	coronary care unit
	chronic sick and spinal injury
	psychiatry and drug and alcohol
	Total – 1044 beds

Clinical services:	accident and emergency
	operating theatres – 12 suites
	diagnostic X-ray, scanning and Nuclear Magnetic Resonance (NMR)
	radiotherapy, nuclear medicine
	haemodialysis
	laboratory
	cardiac investigation

It is often said that every new hospital is out of date the moment it is built. Hospitals take so long to design and build that this is often the case. One answer to this problem of premature obsolescence is a building providing 'universal space', that is a series of structurally uninterrupted floors, to which services such as air-conditioning ducts, pipes and cables could be brought from above, and from which waste could be taken from below. There is no need to zone the functions. Departments can be placed anywhere at any time during the life of the building.

These ideas were incorporated in a modular building systems design by the late George Agron of SMP for the Veterans' Administration (VA). In the late 1960s the VA mounted a major hospital building programme. The Houston Medical Center is the latest and largest of these buildings.

The VA hospitals provide comprehensive health care for ex-servicemen and their families. In addition to a wide range of acute medical and surgical specialties the Houston center provides extensive long-term care: psychiatry, treatment for drug/alcohol addiction and spinal injury and geriatric medicine. All these facilities are accommodated in one monolithic building of 1.5 million square feet (140,000 m²) constructed in one complete operation.

The earlier VA hospital plans were based on a deep rectangular overall layout. At Houston a more linear form is used. Instead of the square ring circulation pattern a single spine corridor separates the clinical departments from the nursing units. The latter are triangular in plan, similar to the David Grant ward units (see p. 26).

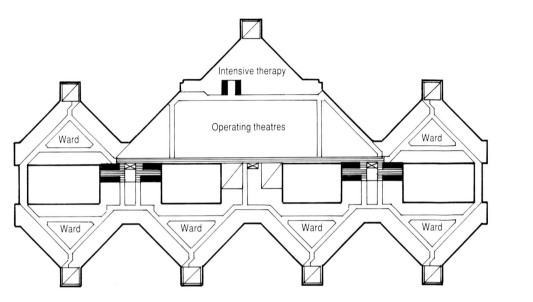

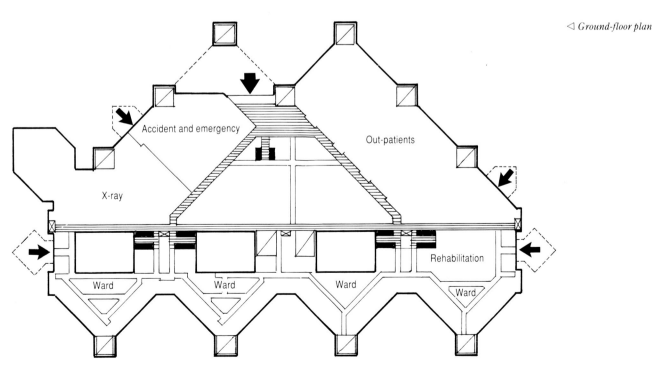

△ View towards main entrance

This triangular form is taken as the basic 'service module' throughout the scheme. Each module comprises a functional floor of approximately 1500 m² together with an interstitial floor. All vertical building elements – columns, stairs, lifts and fire enclosures – are located at the boundaries of the services modules. The main vertical towers, containing plant and feeding ducts down from the roof-top machine rooms, are placed at the external apex of each triangular module.

The innovative high-tech design solution skilfully controls the movement of people, materials and services within a large complex institution that is both adaptable to change and free to grow in the future.

Externally its massiveness is broken up by the undulating plan form and by the elegantly detailed towers. Four large internal landscaped courtyards bring daylight into the patient rooms and the spine corridors.

However it is in the clinical areas on the other side of the spine that the interior appears very much at the mercy of the system. Of some 2000

rooms in this densely planned area, more than half are without daylight or external view.

△ *Aerial perspective showing plant 'modules' rising at intervals between intersections of functional and service floors*

△ *View of staff base in typical ward unit*

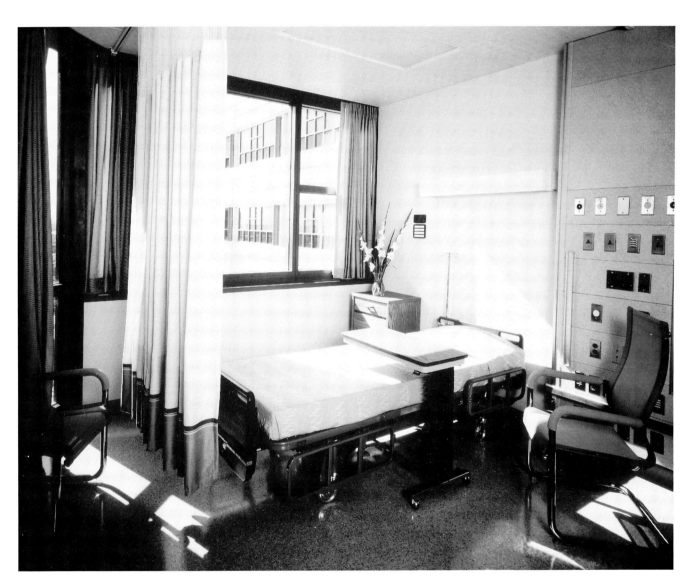

△ *Typical patient's room*

▷ *Typical plant tower*

Mackenzie Health Sciences Center

Edmonton, Alberta

Architects:	**Zeidler Roberts Partnership in association with Groves Hodgson Palenstein and Wood Gardner**
Type:	**university teaching hospital, 940 beds**
Gross floor area:	**170,840 m²**
Area per bed:	**180 m²**
Site:	**redevelopment of existing campus site in two main phases; very restricted; car parking in double basement**
Delivery timescale	**phase 1 completed 1983**
	phase 2 completed 1986

Planning and design summary

Development concept
universal space; interstitial service floors; six storeys; central spine corridor; atriums instead of courts

Functional content

Clinical specialties:	general medicine
	general surgery
	neurosurgery
	cardiology
	ear nose and throat ophthalmology
	intensive therapy
	coronary care
	obstetrics/gynaecology
	paediatrics
	Total – 940 acute beds
Clinical services:	accident and emergency
	operating theatres
	diagnostic X-ray, scanning and NMR
	nuclear medicine
	laboratory
	cardiac investigation
	out-patient clinics

▷ *Aerial view from south-west*

The Mackenzie Health Sciences Center is a 900-bed university teaching hospital and tertiary referral centre for Northern Alberta, the Yukon and North West Territories. The new building is largely a replacement of a number of separate facilities in downtown Edmonton. It was funded from the local oil and gas industries. Two important post-war medical teaching and research facilities – the Clinical Sciences building on the southern boundary, and the Medical Sciences building (Medical School) to the north – are retained.

The new hospital was constructed in two main phases on a very congested site between the two retained existing buildings. The whole of the existing hospital remained fully operational throughout the construction period.

At ground-floor level two off-street main entrances are connected by a broad concourse opening into an enclosed garden atrium, equipped like a shopping mall, with caf'es, shops and banks. Free-standing glass-enclosed lifts rise to five upper floors. The first floor is devoted to teaching and research and includes a pedestrian link running north/south connecting the two existing teaching and research buildings. In-patient wards are located on each of the 2nd to 4th floors with approximately 300 beds per floor. Diagnostic and treatment departments are placed along the central spine corridor and in its projecting tail to the south.

The in-patient wards are planned in 54-bed units along the periphery of the rectangular building.

Each unit contains three sections of 18 beds arranged in one-bed and two-bed rooms each with WC/shower rooms en suite. A unit kitchen, lounge area, offices and central staff base are common to each set of three sections. The original plan envisaged a reduced staff at night covering all three sections and operating from the central staff base. In practice this policy has been rejected by the nursing staff who now use the base only for computer and other support functions.

Approximately one-third of the patient rooms have windows looking into the atrium. Preliminary studies indicate that patients enjoy this dramatic space and like watching the movement of people on the open walkways and terraces. Many prefer this to the street views on the other side of the building.

In designing the McMaster Health Sciences Center, Hamilton, Ontario in 1972, Eberhard Zeidler was one of the first to see the advantage of a universally serviced space in combating premature obsolescence. He persuaded his clients that it was not necessary to wait for final approval of detailed plans before letting a contract. Once his budget had been agreed he could go ahead and build the carcass and main services runs, knowing that they would be adequate for any functional demands. One of the first to use interstitial service floors, McMaster, has been visited by hospital planners from all over the world.

In addition to the rigorous application of these

▽ Cross section showing atrium and interstitial floors

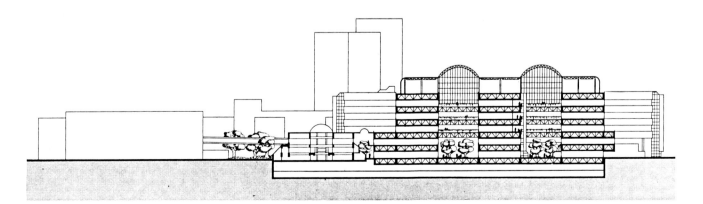

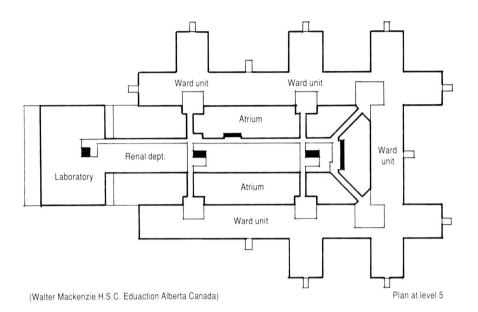

▷ *Plan level 5* (Walter Mackenzie H.S.C. Eduaction Alberta Canada) Plan at level 5

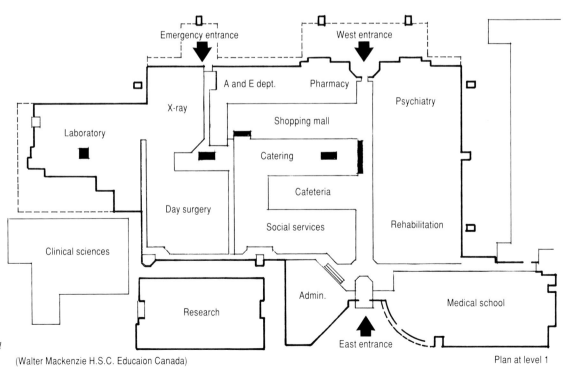

▷ *Plan level 1 (ground floor)* (Walter Mackenzie H.S.C. Educaion Canada) Plan at level 1

principles at the Mackenzie Center, Zeidler
introduces the atrium into hospital building. Instead
of the empty, litter-strewn courtyards, unused in
northern climates, there is a tropical garden with
terraces, pergolas and fountains. Vertical air-
conditioning ducts rise up in brightly coloured tubes
to the full height of the glass-topped space. People
entering the hospital now have something to look at
other than directional signs leading to long grey
corridors unlit by daylight. Clearly, Mackenzie, like
its predecessor McMaster, is a seminal building.

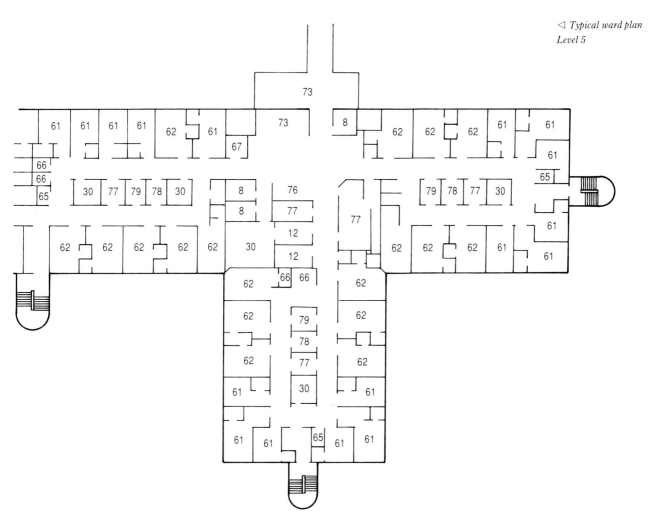

◁ *Typical ward plan*
Level 5

△ *Lecture theatre*

◁ *View of atrium showing
air-conditioning ducts*

▽ *Long section Level 1*

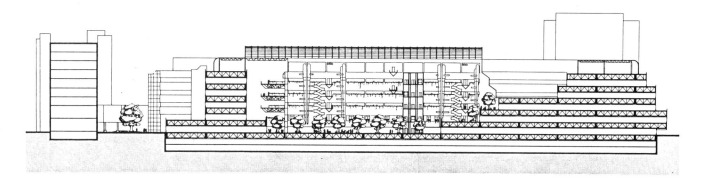

◁ ◁ *Mackenzie Health Sciences Center. View of main entrance*

◁ *View of atrium*

▷ *Mackenzie Health Sciences Center. Typical patient's bedroom*

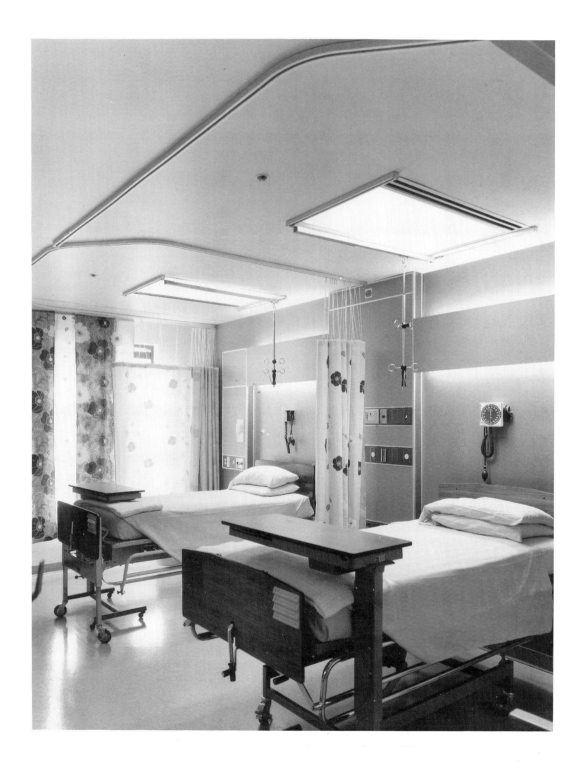

University Teaching Hospital, Essen,
Germany

Architects:	**Heinle, Wischer and Partners, Stuttgart**
Type:	**teaching hospital, new surgical wing, 240 beds**
Gross floor area:	**34,549 m²**
Area per bed:	**N/A**
Site:	**part of existing teaching hospital; steeply sloping site very restricted by existing buildings; parking 124 cars**
Delivery timescale:	**planning commenced 1983 construction started 1985 construction completed 1989 total period, six years**

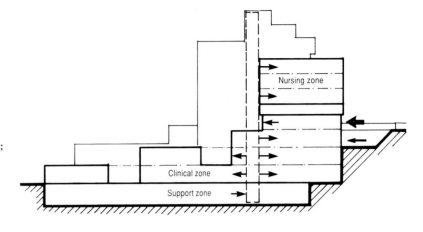

△ *Schematic section note entrances at level midway between nursing and clinical zones*

Planning and design summary

Development concept
vertical zones; seven storeys, tower on stepped podium with landscaped roofs

Functional content

District specialties:	general surgery – 194 beds accident and emergency neurosurgery orthopaedic surgery intensive therapy – 46 beds
Clinical services:	accident and emergency operating theatres – 11 suites diagnostic X-ray laboratory

	rehabilitation surgical out-patient clinics
Teaching:	provision for certain university research and teaching facilities

The University Teaching Hospital and associated teaching and research institutes occupy a large site near the city centre. Some existing buildings date from the early 1900s, others have been added over the years. All are separate structures, apparently isolated, but actually linked together by a network of subways carrying services and supplies. The new facility provides a major new accident and general surgery. It follows the campus tradition, being free-standing and largely self-contained, having a full range of clinical support services.

◁ *Side elevation*

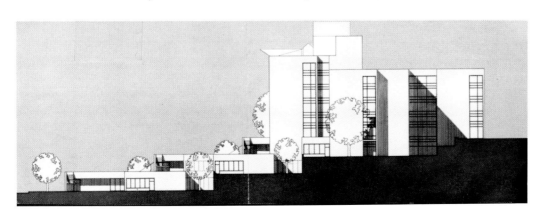

△ *View of nursing tower from stepped podium terrace*

Planning is based on conventional vertical zoning but skilful use of the natural slope of the site has helped to produce a design solution in which the podium becomes part of the landscape and the tower just a four-storey slab.

The main entrance for patients and visitors is approached from the north or campus side. At this level (O) one is exactly half-way up the building midway between the nursing zone (three storeys above) and the clinical zone (three storeys below).

A spacious entrance hall and generous lobbies at all levels give views through a spectacular curved window-wall running the full height of the building above podium level. The descending terraces, formed by the podium roofs, are accessible from the main entrance lobby and step down to street level. The architecture is pure white and cool, both inside and out, with simple but robust detailing of stairways and balustrades.

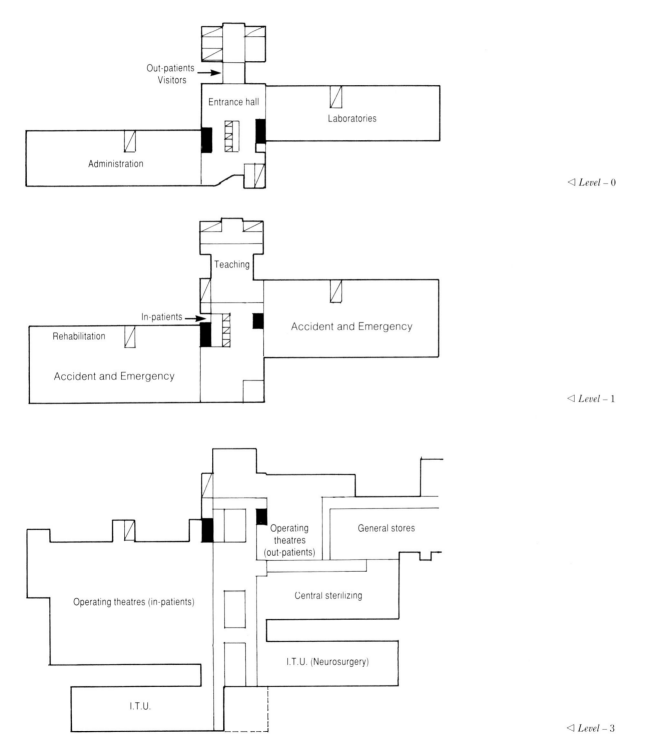

◁ *Level – 0*

◁ *Level – 1*

◁ *Level – 3*

△ *View of courtyard in podium*

▷ *View of main entrance hall and staircase*

University Teaching Hospital, Utrecht

Architects:	**EGM Architects, Dordrect**
Type:	**university teaching hospital, 800 beds, 1400 students**
Gross floor area:	**90,000 m^2**
Area per bed:	**112 m^2**
Site:	**replacement of existing hospital on new site on outskirts of the city**
Delivery timescale:	**planning 1978–80 design 1980–81 construction 1981–89**

△ *Schematic plan showing relationship of zones*

Planning and design summary

Development concept
horizontal zones; five storeys linked by atria and courtyards

Functional content

Specialties:	general medicine
	general surgery
	intensive therapy
	coronary care
	ENT opthalmology
	paediatrics
	obstetrics and gynaecology
	psychiatry
Clinical services:	accident and emergency
	operating theatres
	diagnostic X-ray, scanning, NMR
	radiotherapy and Nuclear Medicines
	out-patient clinics, day hospital
	laboratories
	clinical teaching and research
	blood transfusion service

One of the largest hospital projects to be planned and completed in the 1980s, the Academisch Ziekenhuis Utrecht (AZU) provides facilities for 900 in-patients, 1400 out-patients, 1400 students, and 3000 staff. The work of removing an existing city centre teaching hospital out to a suburban location involved the creation of a complete new infrastructure including direct connection to the A28 motorway, a rail-link, a new bus station with corridor into the hospital entrance concourse and a multi-storey car park with pedestrian bridge to the forecourt.

The management of this vast organization is based on modern concepts of devolved responsibility to clinical management teams for various groups of services. Decisions on patient care and budgets are taken as close as possible to the point of treatment. The needs of the patient, referred to as the client, are paramount and every effort is directed to meeting them including greatly enhanced 'up front' patient services – special reception bureau, patient library, restaurants and cafés with live music, lounges, shops, banks and very generous circulation space. Like the Mackenzie Health Sciences Center, Canada (a primary influence, p. 39) these spaces are in the form of atria: vaulted concourses give access to all facilities used by out-patients, visitors and staff.

A 'percent for art' scheme operates for most new Dutch hospitals. A quarter of 1% of the total construction cost goes towards art embellishments in public spaces. At AZU 18 artists were involved in

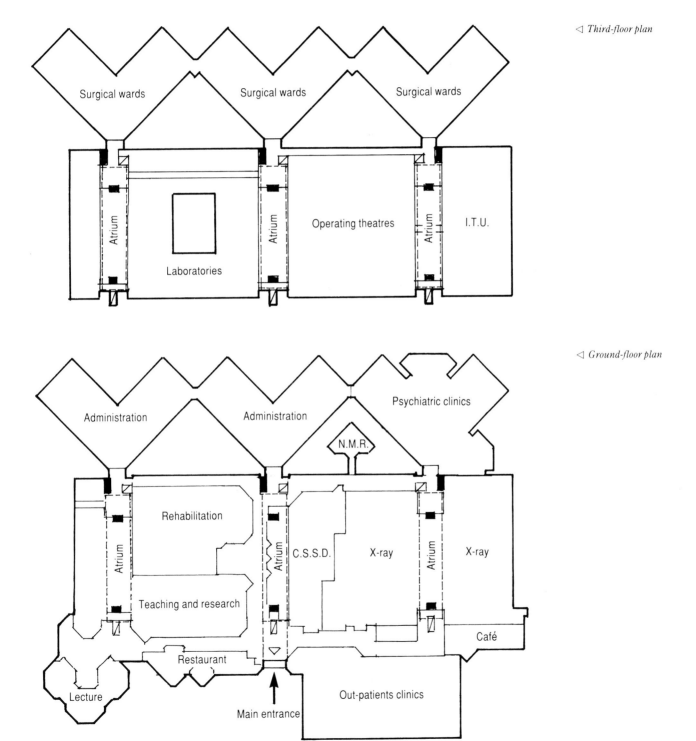

◁ *Third-floor plan*

◁ *Ground-floor plan*

▷ *Main atrium showing cafeteria terraces*

▷▷ *(Above) View towards entrance forecourt showing glazed roof to central atrium*

▷▷ *(Below) View of six-storey ward block*

△ *Entrance concourse*

▷ *Interior view of atrium showing galleried access to department entrances*

various projects including a canopied information desk in the entrance foyer, special floor decorations, acoustic panels suspended in the atria to reduce noise levels, signposting, and interior design and finishes. The emphasis on lavish public spaces contrasts with the narrow austere greyness of many recent UK hospital entrance halls.

External finishes are in dazzling white relieved only by rather thin grey string courses. This treatment is carried through the glass-fronted atria.

The mass of the building is not seen from the entrance forecourt where the clearly visible vaulted forms of the atria, together with the flying pedestrian bridge, gives the familiar appearance of a shopping centre. On the other side, the six-storey ward blocks present a continuous unbroken jagged wall of building reminiscent of 1960s housing.

Central Emergency Hospital, Abu Dhabi

Architects: **HDP (Overseas) Ltd, UK**
Planning
consultant: **Paul James**
Type: **new surgical wing of acute general hospital, 300 beds**
Gross floor area: **52,000 m²**
Area per bed: **173 m²**
Site: **restricted urban site in Abu Dhabi city adjoining existing Al Jazirah Hospital**
Delivery **competition winner 1982**
timescale: **construction commenced 1985 but suspended for three years revised and greatly enlarged scheme approved 1989**

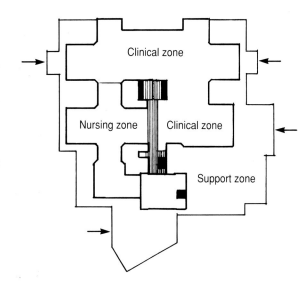

△ *Schematic plan showing relationship of zones*

Planning and design summary

Development concept
horizontal zones linked by central spine corridor; three storeys plus penthouse

Functional content
Specialties: trauma and orthopaedic surgery
general surgery
cardiac surgery
intensive therapy and coronary care unit
Clinical services: accident and emergency centre for Abu Dhabi
operating theatres – eight suites
diagnostic X-ray and scanning
central laboratory for Abu Dhabi
cardiac investigation

The modern city of Abu Dhabi, like others throughout the Gulf, is one of great contrasts. People in traditional dress live and work in Dallas-style buildings which make no reference to Islamic culture or to traditional architecture. However, things are changing, people are becoming concerned that they may have lost their heritage in the headlong rush to modernize along Western lines. The Ministry of Public Works, for instance, are now issuing project briefs to architects insisting that their designs take account of Islamic social and architectural traditions.

The site of the new Central Emergency Hospital borders a street which is now lined with stylish new villas in stone and brick: stalactite capitals support Saracenic pointed, horseshoe, and multifoil arches around colonnaded courtyards and projecting balconies. The new hospital, designed and detailed by Arab architects, will therefore be in context when completed.

Islamic social and religious conventions demand that men and women are appropriately dressed in public. In an acute hospital, receiving and treating emergencies day and night, patients are likely to be in a state of undress. Accordingly the brief called for complete segregation of males and females throughout their stay in hospital.

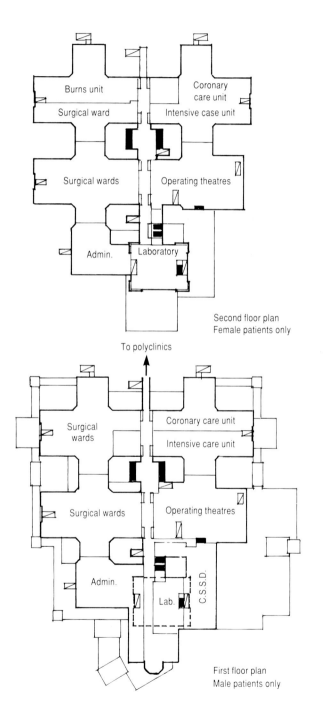

Second floor plan
Female patients only

◁ *Second-floor plan – female patients only*

◁ *First-floor plan – male patients only*

△ *View towards male patient entrance*

The three-storey horizontal design concept allocates a complete floor to each sex – females on the second floor, males on the first floor. Each level is virtually a complete hospital with wards, operating theatres, intensive therapy units (ITUs), laboratory etc.

On the ground floor the primary segregation of male and female admissions is via separate entrances on opposite sides of the building. Two sets of examination, treatment, and resuscitation rooms are separated by a common X-ray department and minor operating theatre suite. Both these departments have separate reception, waiting and toilets. Exam/treatment cubicles are in a radial form around a central staff base to give staff maximum control during busy periods. Immediately inside the two entrances are waiting rooms for relatives of the opposite sex. Relatives visiting patients in the wards enter the hospital through the main entrance at ground level which is also used by staff.

In addition to the large accident department the building accommodates the central diagnostic laboratories for Abu Dhabi. These are planned in the seven-storey tower above the main entrance.

▽ *Elevation*

△ *View of model*

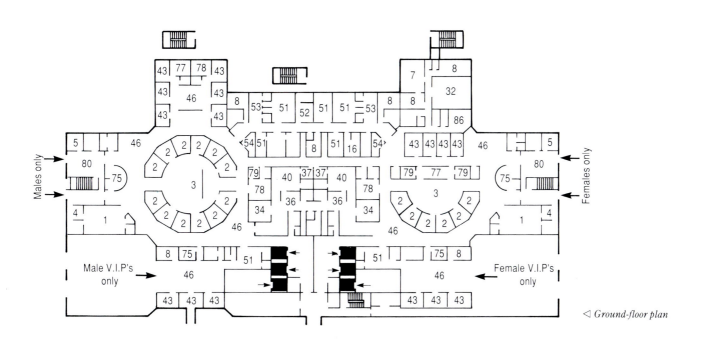

Sri Sathya Sai Institute of Higher Medical Science, Bangalore, South India

Architects:	**Keith Critchlow & Associates, Jon Allen and Triad Architects**
Planning consultant:	**Dr Ann Noble**
Type:	**specialist hospital, 100 beds**
Gross floor area:	**15,000 m²**
Area per bed:	**150 m²**
Site:	**100 miles north of Bangalore in South India, the 50 acre site lies in a well-populated rural area but with adjacent air field.**
Delivery timescale:	**start of planning and design – September 1990 construction started – January 1991 opening – November 1991**

Planning and design summary

Development concept
horizontal zones linked by central spine corridor; single storey

Functional content

Specialties:	cardiology
	cardio-thoracic surgery
	neurology
	urology
	intensive therapy
	coronary care
Clinical services:	operating theatres (six suites)
	day surgery theatres (two suites)
	diagnostic imaging
	cardiac investigation
	renal dialysis
	out-patient clinics

▽ *Panoramic view showing domed central entrance for patients*

This super specialty hospital is the inspired idea of Sri Sathya Sai Baba, the spiritual teacher and guide to millions of people in India and around the world.

The primary guide given by the client was that the architecture should be 'strong, beautiful and comfortable'. Further, the Institute was envisioned to be a model of health care provision, both in its combination of beauty of design with latest medical equipment and in its encouragement of the highest standards of medical services and expertise allied with the provision of free care to the rural poor. The initial medical brief was supplied by Dr A N Safaya. Located away from an urban centre the project included the contribution of all necessary supporting infrastructure, including staff housing and aimed to minimize the reliance on imported resources. The large site allowed the medical facilities to be on ground level, and tall ceilings

encouraged maximum use of natural ventilation. Both these measures minimized energy usage and reliance, and allowed patients to be close to the curative efforts of the natural world. The planning of the site was also influenced by the recognition that flexibility was crucial for future expansion as well as ongoing design development, as construction started in January 1991, no more than 5 months after initial briefing, in order to achieve the opening of Phase 1, the cardiology specialty, on 23 November 1991.

The internal planning of the Institute has all departments, with their own internal circulation, reached from the main street corridor, whose gentle curve and frequent enclosed courtyards are designed to afford the patients and staff orientation and inspiration. It is fundamental to the design philosophy that Beauty is intrinsic to each detail in

▽ *View of loggia at end of ward wing*

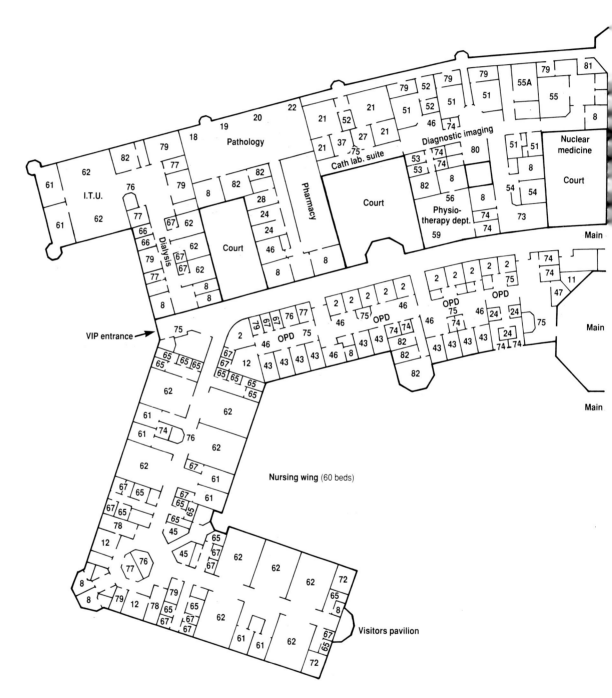

the knowledge that it inspires the will to recover.

The design procedure was conducted on the conviction that a truly health promoting building is one which integrates at every level the practical, clinical and medical necessities with a sense of proportion, beauty and space in which both familiarity (a word closely connected to family) and unfamiliarity can co-exist. The design intention is to

◁ *Ground floor plan*

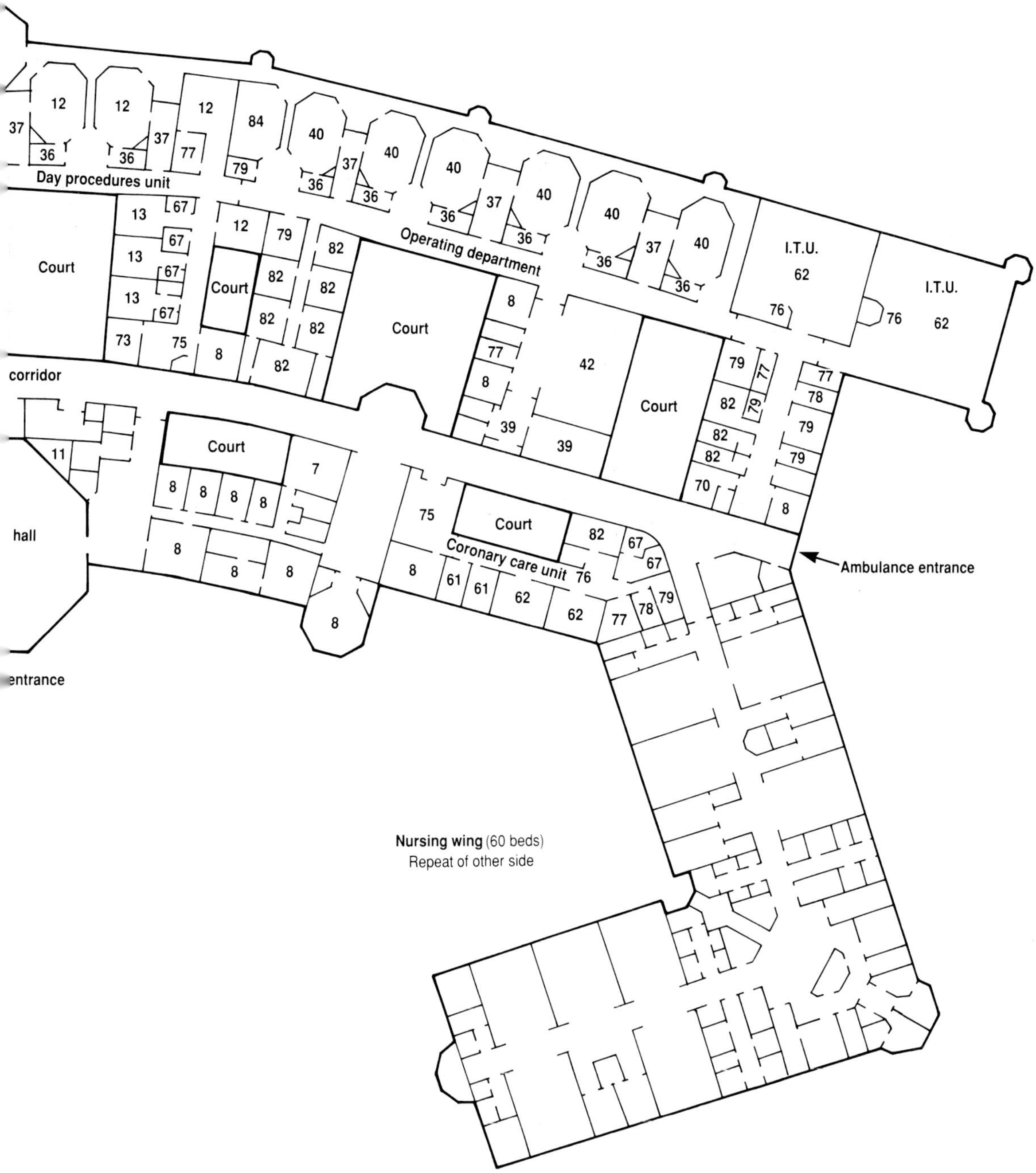

Day procedures unit

Court

corridor

hall

entrance

Operating department

Court

Court

I.T.U.
62

I.T.U.
62

Court

Court

Coronary care unit

Ambulance entrance

Nursing wing (60 beds)
Repeat of other side

minimize fear and maximize recovery with understanding between patients and staff. Special provision for visitors, carefully planned gardens and fountain courts all express the acknowledgement of the founding idea that there is no separation between body, soul and spirit or an individual and their family and social context.

Chelsea and Westminster Hospital, Chelsea

Architects:	**Sheppard Robson, London**
Type:	**teaching hospital, 665 beds**
Site:	**city block in central London**
Delivery timescale:	**design 1987–88**
	construction commenced 1989
	completion 1992

Planning and design summary

Functional content
665 acute beds; full range of specialties: accident and emergency, obstetric and children's departments, day surgery unit, psychiatric department, ITU and coronary care, operating theatres

Development concept
universal space, six storeys with central atrium

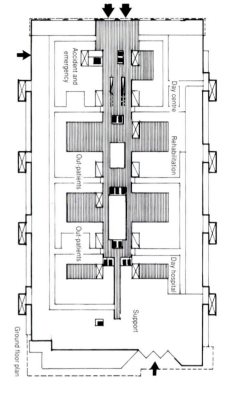

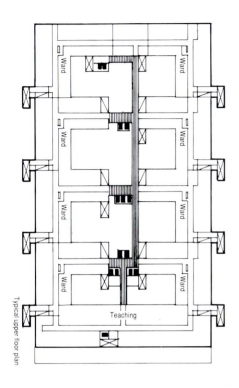

Typical upper floor plan

RICHARD CARMAN 10/90

The only complete London teaching hospital to be built in recent years, the new Westminster and Chelsea Hospital is part of a health service rationalization programme in west London. It is partly funded by the sale of long established acute hospital sites located in the midst of the fashionable and expensive residential areas of Chelsea and Kensington. The site occupies a whole city block between Victorian terrace housing with a main frontage on a busy shopping street.

The development is influenced by recent North American and Dutch schemes (see pp. 25–9, 53ff). A six-storey rectangular building with basement car parking covers most of the site. Plastic-roofed atria, instead of courtyards, provide daylight to inward facing rooms. However, unlike many atrium schemes, the building is naturally ventilated. Air intakes below the lower ground-floor level allow air to circulate upwards (via the stack effect) and out through adjustable louvres at roof level. It is claimed that this 'natural' system will both save energy and avoid sick building syndrome. Another innovation is the design of the atria roofs. The fire safety authority was concerned that smoke would collect in the atria. The answer was a roof which will vapourize at high temperatures. Indeed fire safety appears as a major factor in the design. Compare the number of escape stairs with those in the North American and Dutch examples.

△ *Artist's impression of atrium. Note open 'walkways' instead of long dreary main corridors*

The Hospital for Sick Children, Great Ormond Street, Holborn

Architects: **Powell Moya and Partners, London**

Type: **teaching hospital – postgraduate paediatrics, new extension, 120 beds**

Site: **part of existing site (5.9 acres) in central London**

Gross floor area: **18,150 m²**

Delivery timescale: **planning/design 1986–90**
construction 1990–93
completion 1993

Planning and design summary

Functional content
onocology, surgery, haematology, dermatology, bone marrow unit, ITU, operating theatres

▽ *Aerial view of model*

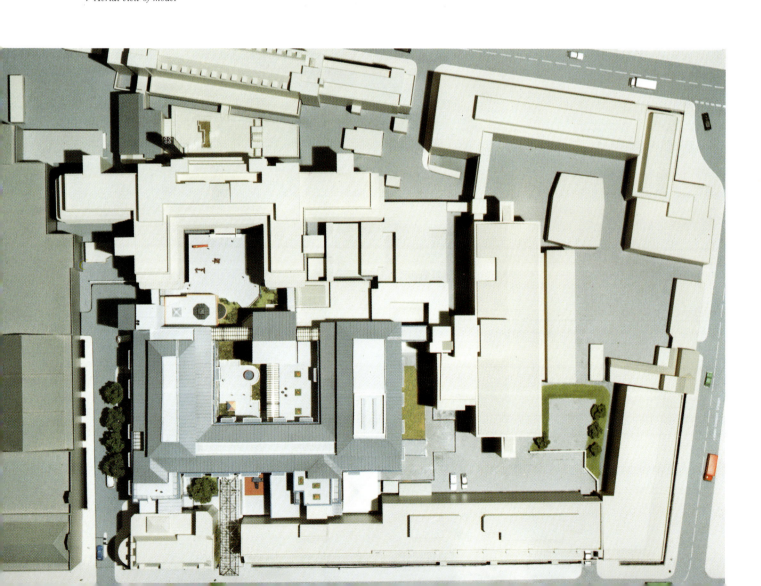

Founded in 1852, Great Ormond Street Children's Hospital is a world-renowned centre of excellence for child health, and the leading UK teaching hospital for paediatrics.

Funded partly by public donations following the 'Wishing Well' appeal in 1985, the new development is aimed at bringing the hospital up to modern standards by building a new extension followed by major up-grading of existing buildings. Much needed facilities for mothers who wish to stay with their children will be provided, together with special units for the treatment of cancer and infectious diseases.

The existing buildings include the original Victorian structure (E.M. Barry, 1875), a nine-storey ward block (1930) and a recently completed eight-storey cardiac block. A major part of the old building has been demolished to leave a clear site between the backs of the buildings fronting Great Ormond Street and the 1930s block. This process involved the moving of the Victorian 'Byzantine' style chapel to a new position on the site.

The new complex is a five-six-storey U-shaped block linked into the existing buildings by a new spine corridor and lift system. It has frontages on Great Ormond Street (set back) and Powis Place. No attempt is made to match the style of the Barry building. Instead light coloured brick panels with dark blue brick string courses are used in conjunction with projecting white aluminium panels.

Inside much is being made of child-centred decorative art. The wards will have themed murals (jungle, sea, countryside etc.). Each ward is to be named after an animal, whose footprints are etched into the floor leading to the ward entrance.

▽ View of architect's model showing elevations to Powis Place

Guy's Hospital, Southwark

Architects:	**Watkins Gray International, Architects**
Type:	**teaching hospital; new extension, 279 beds**
Site:	**part of existing site in central London, 1.6 acres**
Gross floor area:	**50,000 m²**
Delivery timescale:	**currently under construction planning/design 1984–88 construction commenced 1989**

▷▷ *View of model*

Planning and design summary

Functional content
general medicine, general surgery, cardiology, thoracic medicine, renal, specialist out-patient clinics, psychiatric, geriatric, rehabilitation, laboratories, teaching and research

▽ *Perspective view of new development on St Thomas's Street*

This famous London teaching hospital has been progressively rebuilt over the last 50 years (see photograph opposite).

The latest extension, to be known as Phillip Harris House, has largely been funded from endowments and donations.

The site, probably the most over-developed hospital site in the UK, is dominated by Guy's Tower, which, together with New Guy's House, contains the bulk of the 800 beds and supporting services. The new development of over 50,000 m² covers the whole of a 1.6 acre site lying between the tower and the St Thomas's Street frontage.

The plan integrates the extensive out-patient clinics (previously housed in an old isolated building) with their related diagnostic and treatment services located at the base of the tower. At the same time new day facilities for surgery, renal medicine and cardiology are included. The building is six storeys high and is planned round a series of glass-roofed atria. The design, based on an earlier outline scheme by the neo-classical architect John Simpson, seeks to restore the line of St Thomas's Street (which had been destroyed by the tower) and to maintain the character of the listed Guy's House and the façades of the Victorian railway sheds opposite.

◁ *Guy's Tower c. 1975*

◁ *New Guy's House c. 1960*

▷ *New Phillip Harris House c. 1990*

▷ *Guy's House 18th–19th century*

Regional General Hospitals

Etela-Pohjanmaa Central Hospital, Seinajoki,
    Finland

Vrinnevis Hospital, Norrk.oping, Sweden

The Royal Hospital, Oman

Cuzco Hospital, Peru

Etela-Pohjanmaa Central Hospital, Seinajoki

Architects:	**Veijo Martikainen, Helsinki**
Type:	**acute general hospital, 558 beds**
Gross floor area:	**68,000 m²**
Area per bed:	**122 m²**
Site:	**large sloping site bordering a lake in south-west Finland**
Delivery timescale:	**completed in three phases 1972–83**

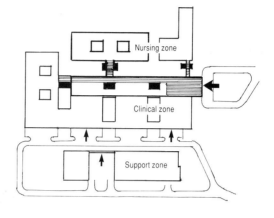

◁ *Schematic plan showing relationship of zones*

Planning and design summary

Development concept
horizontal zones; four storeys; entrances on all four levels

Functional content

Specialties:
general surgery – 160 beds
general medicine – 120 beds
obstetrics and gynaecology – 109 beds
paediatric – 60 beds
ENT – 28 beds
opthalmology – 26 beds
neurology – 40 beds
dermatology – 15 beds
intensive therapy

Clinical services:
accident and emergency
out-patients' clinics
operating theatres
diagnostic X-ray
laboratory
rehabilitation
obstetric delivery and premature baby unit
day-care centre

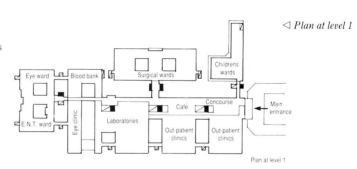

◁ *Plan at level 1*

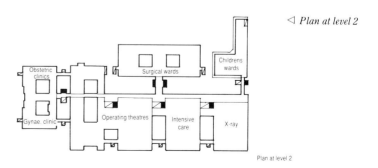

◁ *Plan at level 2*

△ *Landscaped courtyard*

One of the newest of the 21 central acute general hospitals in Finland, Etela-Pohjanmaa is the first to have been based on the horizontal zoning strategy and to have been delivered in a series of fully operational phases.

Now fully completed the hospital serves a population of 194,000 people with an average stay of 7.7 days per patient. Out-patient attendances total 104,000 per annum.

Built on a large open stretch of land sloping down towards a beautiful lake, the design is based on the 'spine-and-pavilion' principle, similar to a number of recently completed provincial UK schemes.

A central main corridor bisects the slope of the land; on one side, overlooking the spectacular lake, is the nursing zone; on the other, a series of pavilions projecting at right angles accommodate

the clinical departments. Separate entrances for in-patient admissions, visitors, out-patients and supplies are on four different levels.

Landscaped courtyards separate the ward blocks from the central spine corridors at the two upper levels. A gap between the former allows views across the lake when walking down the long straight corridor.

All parts of the complex are built in reinforced concrete frames, cast *in situ*, and rendered externally. Roofs are uniformly flat and featureless giving the hospital a somewhat dated Modernist appearance. However the colouring, pale yellow vertical elements against snow white façades, together with the superb natural setting, gives it a welcoming and humane character.

△ *View across the lake*

▷▷ *Main entrance forecourt*

Vrinnevis Hospital, Norrköping

Architects:	**Bo Castenfors Arkiktektkontor, Stockholm**
Type:	**acute general hospital, 480 beds**
Gross floor area:	**100,000 m²**
Area per bed:	**208 m²**
Site:	**large parkland site 3 km from the town centre**
Delivery timescale:	**construction commenced 1982 construction completed 1987**

Planning and design summary

Development concept
campus type development; zones linked by single storey corridors; maximum three storeys

Functional content

Specialties:	general medicine – 132 beds
	general surgical – 84 beds
	orthopaedic – 84 beds
	obstetrics and gynaecology – 72 beds
	ENT – 22 beds
	ophthalmology – 15 beds
	paediatric – 36 beds
	infectious diseases – 35 beds
	intensive therapy
Clinical services:	operating theatres
	diagnostic X-ray and scanning
	laboratory
	obstetric delivery and premature baby unit
	rehabilitation
	out-patients' clinics
	accident and emergency

▷ *Bird's eye view showing relationship of zones*

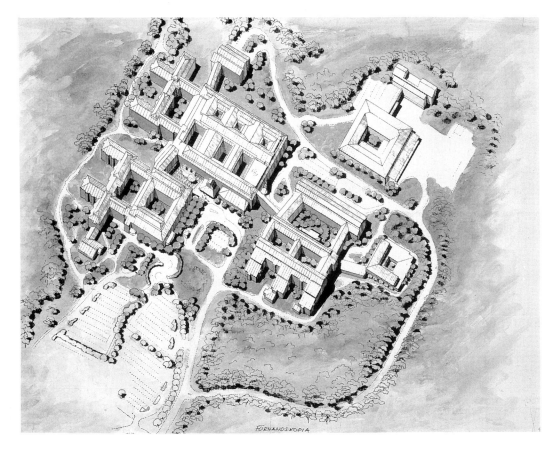

▷▷ *Elevation*

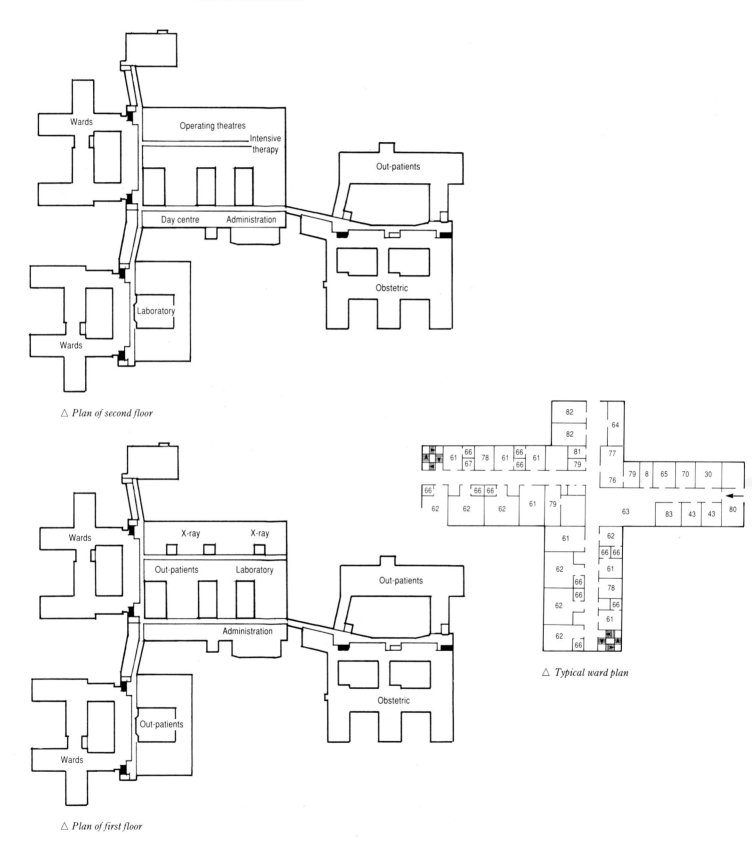

△ *Plan of second floor*

△ *Plan of first floor*

△ *Typical ward plan*

▷ *Lounge/dining room in typical ward*

An alternative to the integrated or monolithic whole hospital plan is the university campus or village concept in which a number of loosely knit independent structures, each containing a group of specialties, are linked at ground level by a wide corridor or 'street'. These semi-isolated buildings contain groups of related specialties e.g. medical/ surgical, obstetrics/paediatrics, cardio-thoracic, neuro-sciences, etc. all with their own clinical support services. They are linked by the street to common support services such as catering, stores, pharmacy etc. Such a scheme requires a great deal of land but it does have important advantages. First, it allows the hospital, in the words of John Weeks, 'to grow with order and change with calm'. Second, the breaking down of the content into smaller pieces can result in a more humane architectural treatment. Like a town or village, each group of structures, including the main street itself, is capable of separate growth in response to changing future demands.

At Vrinnevis, a large site on the outskirts of the town of Norrköping, the superb natural landscape is ideal for this type of development. No building is more than three storeys or exceeds the height of the many fine trees surrounding the building.

The main entrance is in the centre of the 'village'. Nearby, but screened by the trees, are stops for trams, buses and taxis. From here the street leads off to the medical and surgical blocks on one side and to the mothers' and childrens' units on the other.

The three-storey ward blocks are arranged around gardens with easy access from the ground-floor wards.

Adult ward units each of 28 beds, in four-bed, two-bed and one-bed rooms, are linked in pairs by common facilities for staff and a balcony for

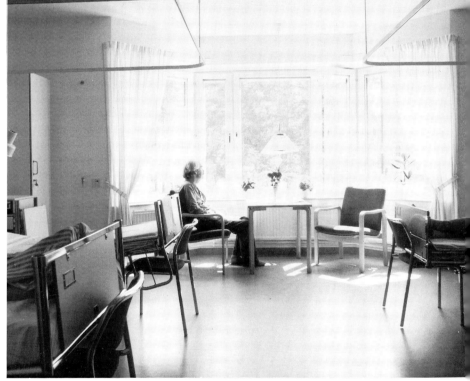

▷ *(Middle) Typical four-bed patients' room (view towards bay window)*

▷ *Staff base in centre of ward*

▷ View of typical ward block

▽ View towards main entrance

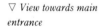

patients. All four-bed rooms have a wide bay window for sitting-up. The staff base in the centre of the ward is well placed as a control point for the three short corridors leading from the entrance and to the patient rooms.

The architects have consistently carried through their humane concept of the hospital. The informal, seemingly haphazard, relationships between the various blocks, the use of brick cladding, small domestic scale windows, pitched roofs and the romantic landscaping, all contribute to an impression that this is a familiar high-quality housing park. It is certainly very different from the massive multi-storey slab standing on acres of flat-roofed podium, which characterizes the typical modern Swedish hospital.

△ *Landscaped courtyards*

◁ *One of the many garden
courtyards*

The Royal Hospital, Sultanate of Oman

Architects: **George Wimpey International with Percy Thomas Partnership Architects**

Type: **acute general hospital, 629 beds**

Gross floor area: **64,000 m^2**

Area per bed: **102 m^2**

Site: **large desert site on outskirts of Muscat**

Delivery timescale: **planning 1982 design and construction 1983–87 total contract period 43 months**

Planning and design summary

Development concept
horizontal zones; three storeys; deep planning, totally air-conditioned

Functional content

Specialties: general medicine – 306 beds
general surgery – 306 beds
obstetrics – 116 beds
premature baby unit – 30 cots
paediatrics – 28 beds
intensive therapy unit – 36 beds
coronary care unit – 36 beds
private and VIP – 28 beds

Clinical services: operating theatres
diagnostic X-ray and scanning
rehabilitation
obstetric delivery suite
laboratory
renal dialysis
out-patients' clinics
accident and emergency

▷ *Schematic plan showing relationship of zones*

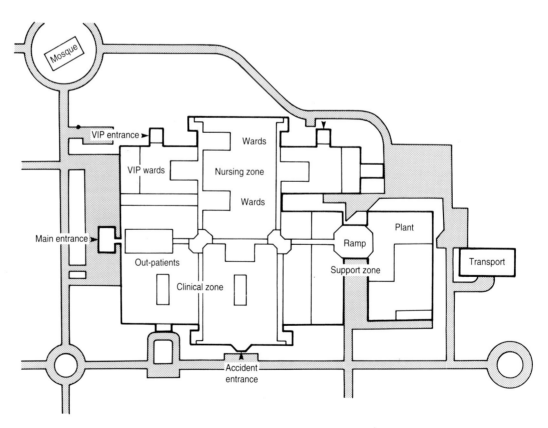

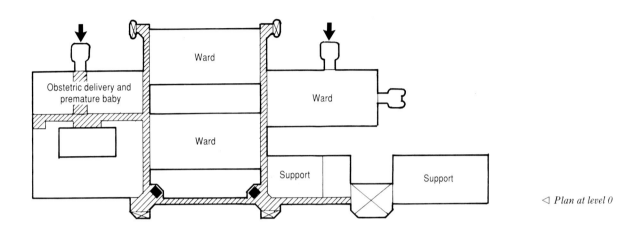

◁ Plan at level 0

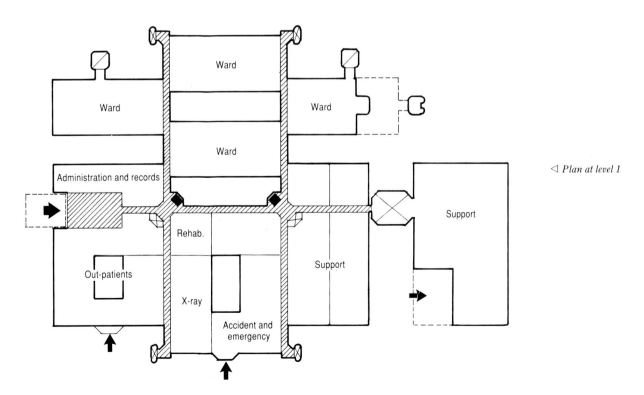

◁ Plan at level 1

△ *View towards main
entrance*

A British 'turnkey' package deal, the Royal Hospital was designed, built and equipped by a consortium led by George Wimpey International, in a total period of only 43 months. All the design work was done in the UK. The construction programme was achieved despite a barren and isolated site with no existing roads or main services. The 2500 workforce had to be housed and fed while working in temperatures of up to 46°C. The entire building is air-conditioned and incorporates one of the largest and most sophisticated central chilling stations designed for a hospital anywhere.

A comprehensive health services plan was prepared by the UK Department of Health in 1982. It involved a detailed survey and assessment of existing health facilities in and around Muscat, the capital city.

A simple horizontally-zoned development plan incorporates deep-planned built forms linked by a central spine corridor at three main levels. Obstetrics and childrens' departments, together with a separate entrance, are on the lower level (level 0). The main entrance, accident and emergency, out-patients' clinics and radiology are on the middle level together with the medical wards. The upper level accommodates all adult surgical wards, ITU and coronary care, and operating theatres. Two banks of lifts serve all patient movement; supplies are moved by trolleys via a spiral ramp direct to each level from the support departments.

The design of the wards takes account of social customs whereby patients' relatives stay in the hospital and attend to the patients. The projecting domed staircase towers provide access to peripheral ward corridors so that the work of the ward staff is not interrupted by the large number of relatives.

Both externally and within the lavish public spaces, there is reference to traditional Islamic architecture and design. Arabesque screens and wall decorations, marble and mosaics, pools and fountains, are everywhere. The three-storey glass-topped entrance hall with open galleries is particularly impressive.

△ One of the domed stairway towers

*△ ▽ Two views of the
main entrance hall*

◁ Main entrance at night

◁ General view of hospital

Cuzco Regional Hospital, Cuzco, Peru

Architects:	**Cooper, Grana, Nicolini, Lima, Peru**
Planning consultant:	**Robert Chapman**
Type:	**acute general hospital, 314 beds**
Gross floor area:	**39,072 m²**
Area per bed:	**78 m²**
Site:	**large site in centre of city, sloping from west to east**
Delivery timescale:	**completed 1986**

Planning and design summary

Development concept
vertical zones; interstitial floor between nursing and clinical zones; three storeys including basement level

Functional content

Specialties:	general medicine – 90 beds
	general surgery – 60 beds
	gynaecology – 30 beds
	obstetrics – 59 beds
	paediatrics – 57 beds
	intensive therapy – 18 beds
Clinical services:	accident and emergency
	diagnostic X-ray
	operating theatres
	delivery suites
	premature baby unit
	rehabilitation
	laboratory
	teaching and training

Early in the 1960s Le Corbusier published a project for a hospital in Venice. Two huge decks, one above the other, were placed over the site, which was mainly water. The upper deck contained all the in-patient wards: clinical departments were on the lower deck with access from both land and water. At a time when the tower-on-podium concept dominated hospital planning, the idea had little influence.

In the 1960s Sheila Clibbon, an English architect, and Martin Sachs, an American clinician, took these ideas a stage further. Between the clinical level and the nursing level they inserted a third 'industrial' floor to accommodate all the support services – catering, supplies, linen stores, mechanical and electrical plant etc.

Cuzco is the first complete hospital to be planned along these lines, except that the middle level is an interstitial service floor only; storage and processing departments being in a basement. Cuzco is a city of great character; the low lying city centre is packed with traditional buildings of not more than four storeys with clay-tiled roofs which are clearly visible from the surrounding higher parts of the town. The local conservation body, The 'Institute Nacional de Cultura', insisted on the building being restricted to a maximum of four storeys and on the use of clay-tiled roofs.

The concept of placing all in-patient wards (over 300 beds) on the top level has been fully exploited by the architects. Planned in a series of L-shaped units linked together around small patios, all the wards enjoy natural light, ventilation and an external view. This arrangement helps to break up

▷ *Schematic section showing relationship of zones*

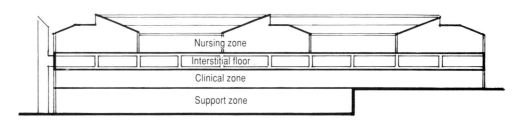

the extensive roof-scape. The scale is further reduced by the use of sloping roofs and clerestory windows to light internal rooms and even corridors. The eaves are brought right down to shield the windows around the patios. The whole effect is one of lightness and domestic scale.

The diagnostic and treatment services are compactly planned on the lower level below the wards. Most of these departments are air-conditioned.

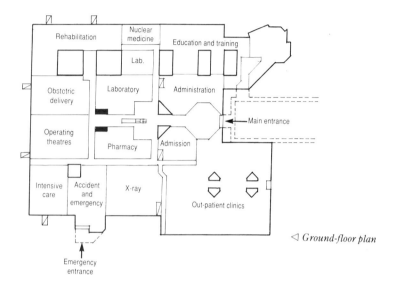

◁ Ground-floor plan

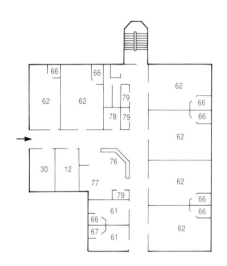

△ Typical ward plan

0 1 2 3 4 5   10   15

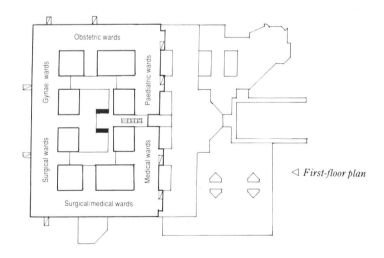

◁ First-floor plan

▽ Long section

On each side of the colonnaded entrance forecourt are projecting single-storey wings; one of these houses the out-patient clinics. Here again the roof is skilfully manipulated to introduce light and air into a deep planned area. The long side elevations are broken up by vertical shafts housing staircases and service ducts and by the jagged roof lines.

Between the two main levels is the interstitial services floor providing space for engineering plant and services feeding both floors.

The main functional disadvantage of the basically vertical concept is that all in-patient journeys, from wards to operating theatres, X-ray and rehabilitation departments, are dependent on lifts. In the developing countries this can pose problems due to poor electro-mechanical maintenance facilities.

◁ *Part south-east elevation*

▽ *Outpatients' main concourse*

▷ *Main entrance forecourt*

▷ *View towards emergency entrance with single-storey out-patients block in foreground*

△ (Left) Detail of roofs
with walkway in
foreground

△ (Right) Corridor on
ward floor. Note
daylighting

▷ Typical six-bed patients'
room

92

District General Hospitals

Scottsdale Memorial Hospital – USA

Melilla District Hospital – Spain

Neukölln District Hospital – Germany

Bad Sackingen District Hospital – Germany

Merwede General Hospital – The Netherlands

Homerton Hospital – UK

Conquest Hospital – UK

West Dorset Hospital – UK

Stoke-on-Trent Hospital – UK

St Mary's Hospital IOW – UK

West Fife Hospital – UK

Scottsdale Memorial Hospital

North Scottsdale, Arizona

Architects:	**NBBJ Group, Seattle**
Type:	**acute general hospital, 120 beds**
Gross floor area:	**14,770 m²**
Area per bed	**123 m²**
Site:	**flat desert land; 38.5 acres about 8 miles from Scottsdale town centre**
Delivery timescale	**construction commenced 1982 completed 1984**

Planning and design summary

Development concept
horizontal zones united by primary spine corridor; three storeys; planned future extension of nursing zone up to 500 beds

Functional content

District specialties:	general surgery
	accident and emergency
	general medical – 98 beds
	intensive therapy – 12 beds
	coronary care
	intermediate care

Clinical services:	accident and emergency
	operating theatres – four suites
	diagnostic X-ray – four rooms
	laboratory
	rehabilitation

In the past decade hospital design in the USA has moved away from the vertical 'tower-on-podium' strategies developed by hospital planning consultants such as Gordon Friesen during the 1950s and 1960s. New nursing methods, more stringent fire and safety codes and increasingly complex electromechanical services have highlighted the need for a more flexible hospital chassis that can grow and change over a time with the least cost and disruption.

Economic constraints and new funding methods prohibit the building of hospitals as complete entities. Strategies that will permit incremental development have led directly to more organic concepts involving dense low rise structures serviced by 'spine' corridors and horizontal ducts. Scottsdale Memorial Hospital is an outstanding example of this new approach. Located in the desert, the new facility works as a satellite of the main hospital in downtown Scottsdale where site

▷ *Schematic plan showing relationships of zones and possible future extensions*

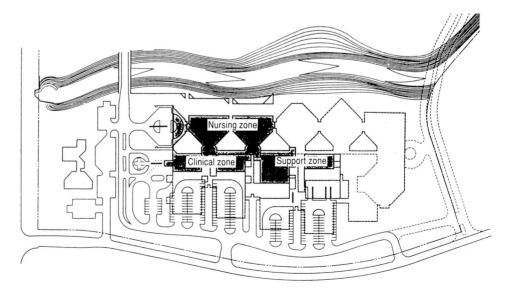

constraints prohibit further development. The first phase provides 120 beds. Expansion to 500 beds can be accomplished, with minimum disruption, by adding nursing units along one side of the spine, and by additions to the clinical zone on the other.

In keeping with the south-west regional heritage and the traditional architectural style in the desert area, the building mass is low and solid: a reflection of the striking natural formations surrounding the hospital. A warm, neutral colour scheme is used both inside and out. Landscaping in the patios and courtyards suggests oases in the desert.

Sun and heat control were a major consideration. No windows face directly west.

Patients' bedrooms are clustered behind an outer wall sunscreen, shielding the rooms from the intense summer sun and giving depth and character to the façades. Exterior wall openings on the east, north and south take advantage of mountain vistas and courtyard views while limiting harsh solar penetration.

The entire building is fully air-conditioned with zoned plant rooms for reheat system and energy conservation thermal transfer equipment.

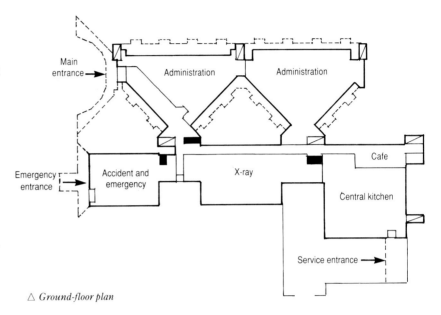

△ *Ground-floor plan*

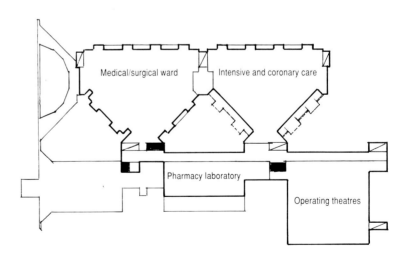

△ *First-floor plan*

△ *View of ward block from*
north-east. Photograph:
Peter Aaron (Esto)

△ *View of clinical block*
from courtyard.
Photograph: Peter Aaron
(Esto)

District Hospital, Melilla

Architects:	**Alfonso Casares Avila and Reinaldo Ruiz Yebenes**
Type:	**acute general hospital, 170 beds**
Gross floor area:	**13,440 m²**
Area per bed:	**80 m²**
Site:	**restricted site near town centre**
Delivery timescale:	**planning 1983–84 construction 1984–88 total period five years**

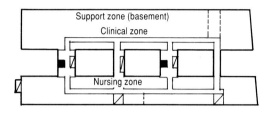

△ *Schematic plan*

Planning and design summary

Development concept
horizontal zones; three storeys

Functional content

District specialties:	general medicine – 42 beds
	general surgery – 64 beds
	obstetrics and gynaecology – 32 beds
	paediatric – 26 beds
	intensive therapy – six beds
Clinical services:	accident and emergency
	operating theatres – four suites
	diagnostic X-ray – five rooms
	laboratory
	obstetric delivery suite
	day centre – haemodialysis
	rehabilitation

In the 1980s the Ministry of Health carried out a major hospital building programme at record speed. Small- and medium-sized (up to 400 beds) acute general hospitals serving up to 150,000 people were planned, designed and constructed in periods of three to five years – remarkably short when compared to the seven to 15 year timescales of Germany and the UK.

Private sector architects and engineers working with small client groups, led by a doctor, can agree a planning brief in a 'few days'. Plans are highly repetitive and standardized: 90% of the wards, for instance, consist of standard blocks of two-bed rooms each with their own toilet, bed-pan washer and shower.

General arrangement drawings only are prepared by the designers, leaving the successful building contractor to produce detailed working drawings for approval by the architect. Public tenders are invited on the basis of the architects drawings and a detailed performance specification. Selection of these bids takes account of the proposed timescale as well as the costs involved in building.

The new hospital at Melilla is a typical example. A simple compact horizontal zone strategy is used: two parallel three-storey blocks, one housing the wards, the other diagnostic and treatment departments, are linked by stairs, lifts and a pedestrian ramp.

The main entrance is at street level on the ground floor of the ward block; admissions are taken direct by lift to the wards above. Out-patients and day-patients proceed to the first floor of the clinical block via the ramp. The accident and emergency department is at this level, accessible off a side street due to the slope of the site.

A simple, repetitive, but well-proportioned window pattern is set into a white rendered external wall. At intervals full height glass walls reveal the staircases and give views of the courtyards between the two blocks. Inside there is plenty of daylight and fresh air; all rooms in the ward block have windows. Corridor lengths are reduced by the staircase lobbies.

Sections of the ground floor are projected into the forecourt and help to emphasize the entry points.

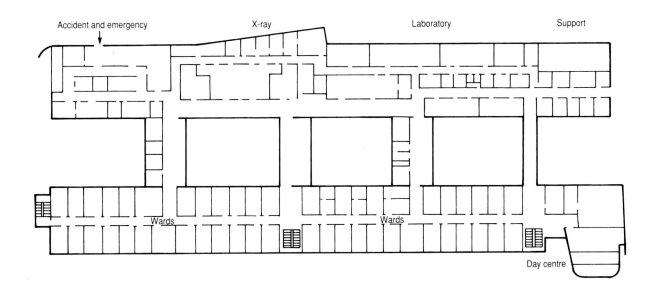

△ *First-floor plan*

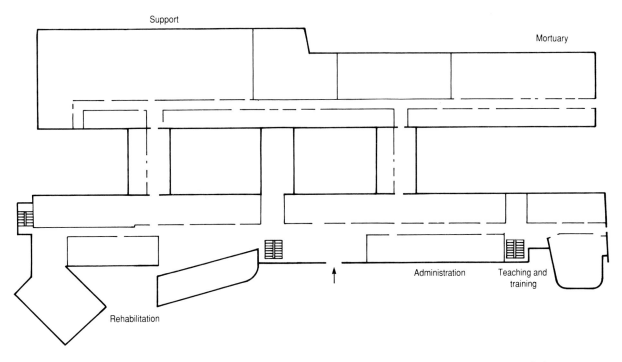

△ *Ground-floor plan*

99

△ *View towards main*
entrance

△ *View of ward block and main entrances*

▷ *Central staircase from courtyard*

District Hospital, Neukölln, Berlin

Architects:	**Professor J.P. Kleihuis in association with Jurgen Konig**
Type:	**acute general hospital, 686 beds**
Gross floor area:	**49,400 m²**
Area per bed:	**72 m²**
Site:	**part of existing hospital site in suburb of Berlin**
Delivery	**competition winner 1973**
timescale:	**design completed 1977**
	completion 1986

Planning and design summary

Development concept
vertical zones; five storeys plus basement

Functional content (New building only)

Specialties:	general medicine – 190 beds
	general surgery – 140 beds
	orthopaedic – 126 beds
	urology – 76 beds
	neurology – 38 beds
	neurosurgery – 38 beds
	intensive therapy
	coronary care – 66 beds
	nuclear medicine – 12 beds
	Total 686 beds
Clinical services:	full range including
	accident and emergency
	radiotherapy and nuclear medicine

The design of this large general hospital, a joint venture between a distinguished urbanist and an experienced hospital architect, was awarded first prize in a competition held in 1973. A major concern was with the orderly regeneration of a part of Berlin which had suffered from the chaotic developments of the 1960s; hastily erected workers housing and welfare homes, unrelated to existing street lines and surroundings.

Over 300 m (985′) long and only 20 m (65′) high, the new hospital is dramatically different from the conventional modern German hospital. It owes more to the finite neo-classical urban schemes of Schinkel than to modern concepts of indeterminacy in hospital design. Four main levels, arranged in two pairs each separated by an engineering sub-floor, house all the medical functions. The lower pair, with external access at both levels, accommodates the clinical zone. The plans are reminiscent of a Greek temple with a central 'Naos' rising through the two floors and lit from a continuous skylight above. A central entrance leads directly into this splendid space. An exposed stairway rises to a gallery on three sides; storey-height murals painted on panels adorn the fourth side. Most departments are directly accessible from this hall which helps to make the elongated plan very compact and functionally efficient.

The entire nursing zone is on the upper two levels, over 300 beds per floor, planned in two parallel linear forms separated by a wide light-well. Two separate banks of lifts and staircases give access to a total of four ward units (150 beds). An ingenious piece of planning, it is very economical in circulation space (a UK nucleus hospital of this length may have a primary circulation corridor some 200 m long).

The interior of the hospital is high-tech, space-age hygiene; gleaming white plastic-faced panels, with immaculately detailed joints, merge into walls and ceilings of similar finishes. The patient bedrooms look like mini operating theatres.

No attempt is made to physically link the new block to the existing 80-year-old hospital (340 beds) above basement level. However, a visual relationship is subtly created by extending the main entrance forecourt into the large landscaped square around which the old pavilion blocks are arranged. Somewhat surprisingly, in view of its classical plan, the architecture of the new building firmly turns its back on tradition in favour of uncompromising high-tech modernism. The façade of the upper two levels is clad in an all-enveloping screen of metal and glass. White laquered aluminium sheets contrast with black profiled aluminium cover strips. Natural linen-weave sun protection shades on natural aluminium frames are independently power operated from controls within the patient rooms.

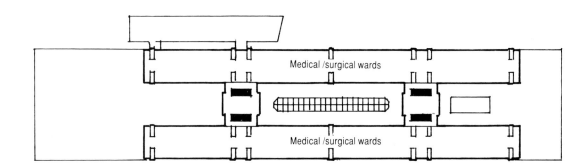

▷ *Plan of typical ward floor*

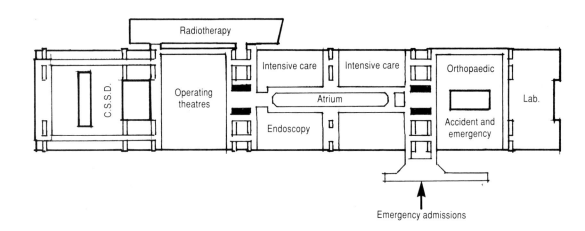

▷ *Plan of first floor*

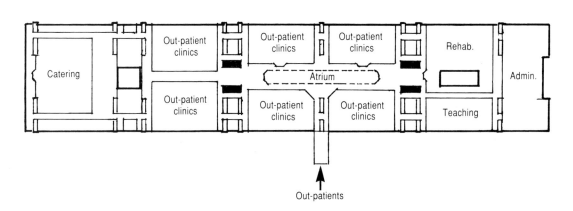

▷ *Plan of ground floor*

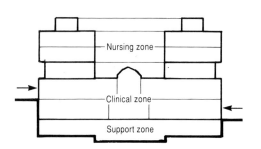

▷ *Schematic section showing relationship of zones*

△ *View of new building; existing hospital in foreground*

▷ *Central hall*

105

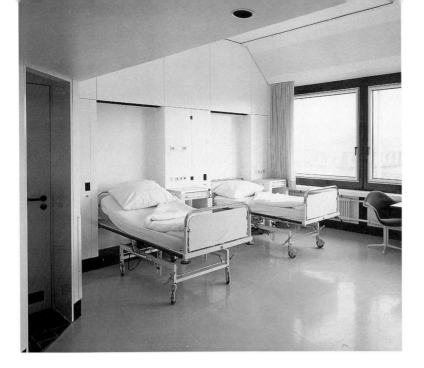

△ *Typical patient bedroom*

▷ *View of glass roof over hall*

◁ *Gallery at first-floor level*

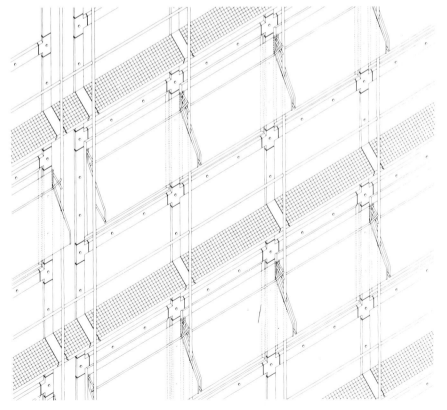

◁ *Detail of external wall*

District Hospital, Bad Sackingen

Architects:	**Heinle, Wischer and Partners, Stuttgart**
Planning consultant:	**Professor Robert Wischer**
Type:	**acute general hospital, 190 beds**
Gross floor area:	**15,500 m²**
Area per bed:	**78.30 m²**
Site:	**gently sloping landscaped grounds of existing sanatorium on outskirts of town; parking for 150 cars**
Delivery timescale:	**competition winner 1972 planning/design completed 1977 construction completed 1979 total period seven years**

Planning and design summary

Development concept
vertical zones; four storeys plus basement; 7.20 m square planning grid

Functional content

District specialties:	general medicine – 64 beds
	general surgery – 74 beds
	obstetrics and gynaecology – 38 beds
	intensive therapy – seven beds
Regional specialties:	ENT and ophthalmic – 15 beds
Clinical services:	accident and emergency
	operating theatres – three suites
	diagnostic X-ray
	rehabilitation
	out-patients' clinics
	laboratory service off–site

In Germany the 1980s saw a period of stagnation in the planning and design of new acute hospitals. Instead, resources were concentrated on the repair and upgrading of existing stock. The major schemes completed during this period were designed in the 1970s after selection on the basis of 'ideas competitions' organized by hospital authorities. Architects were invited to prepare 1:500 scale schematics outlining their ideas. A selection panel of judges drawn from clinicians and administrators, but without advice from architects or engineers, tended to play safe and go for the tried and trusted formula of the tower- or slab-on-podium. Innovation was confined to the shape of the tower and the layout of the nursing units but the basic strategy of vertical zoning was seldom challenged. There are some exceptions, notably at Aachen and Nutingen, both influenced by the McMaster Health Sciences Center, Canada. However, vertical zoning does have a number of functional advantages particularly, as in the more recent German examples, where the tower is flattened into large ward floors on a few levels above the podium.

The small hospital at Bad Sackingen abandons the tower in favour of a low-rise cruciform shape, accommodating over 80 beds per floor, above a ground-level podium. The result is a low-rise building, detailed with typical care and thoroughness in scale with its parkland setting. Inside there is plenty of daylight and views of the landscaped gardens, forecourts and projecting podium roofs.

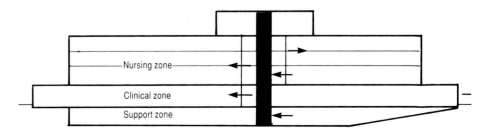

▷ *Schematic section*

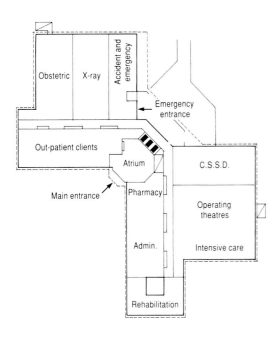

△ *Ground-floor plan*

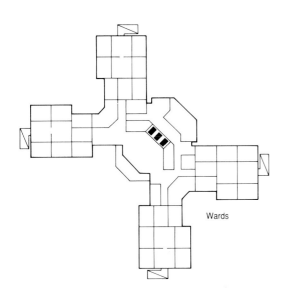

△ *Second-floor plan*

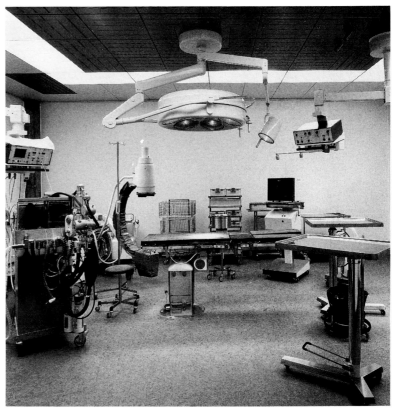

△ *Operating theatre*

Perhaps the great advantage of vertical schemes is their simplicity and economy of circulation. The bank of three lifts at Bad Sackingen serves two lobbies at each level. The front lobby opens to the main entrance hall at ground level. All visitors enter the hospital and use the lifts to gain access to the ward floors where they are received at the respective front lobbies on each floor. Here there is ample waiting space. In-patients use the back lobbies to travel down to the ground floor for treatment and diagnosis. Admissions from the accident and emergency department to the ward also use this route. Finally the lifts travel down to the basement to pick up supplies including patient meals. In this simple way patient, visitor and supplies traffic routes are all segregated without the need for corridors. Compared with most horizontal systems it is very neat and efficient, but everything depends on the lifts.

△ *View of main entrance*
across park

△ *Main entrance foyer*

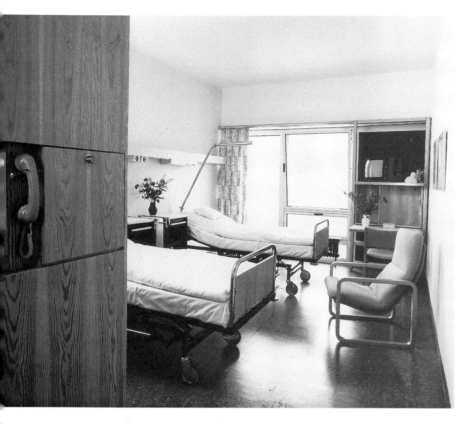

△ *District Hospital, Bad Sackingen. Detail of façade and landscaped roof to podium*

◁ *(Top) Typical patient's bedroom*

◁ *(Bottom) Entrance forecourt*

Merwede General Hospital, Dordrecht

Architects:	**EGM Architecten, Dordrecht**
Type:	**acute general hospital, 390 beds**
Gross floor area:	**32,000 m²**
Area per bed:	**82 m²**
Delivery timescale:	**planning, design commenced 1979**
	completed 1989
	total period ten years

Planning and design summary

Development concept
horizontal zones, four storeys

Functional content

District specialties:	general surgery
	general medicine
	paediatrics
	obstetrics and gynaecology
	accident and emergency
	intensive therapy
	total – 390 beds
Clinical services:	operating theatres
	obstetric delivery
	X-ray
	laboratory
	rehabilitation
	accident and emergency
	day surgery
	out-patients' clinics

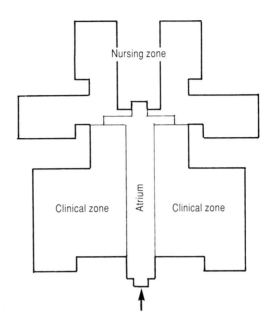

◁ *Schematic plan showing relationship of zones*

Like the University Teaching Hospital, Utrecht, this run-of-the-mill district general hospital uses a straightforward horizontal zoning strategy. Nursing and clinical departments are horizontally contiguous on each of three floors so that in-patient movement patterns are mainly horizontal via a short spine corridor.

▽ *View of ward block*

▷ *Second-floor plan*

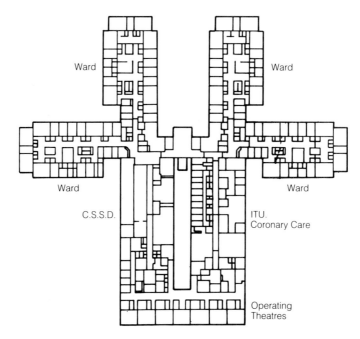

▷ *Ground-floor plan*

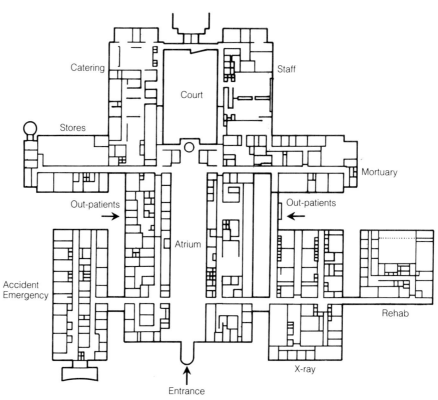

The lower two floors of the clinical block are devoted to out-patient and day-patient services served by a separate circulation system in the form of a wide top-lit arcade running the full length of the block. Access to the first floor is via lifts and a staircase to a gallery over the main entrance. The use of a spacious shopping arcade, instead of the main corridor or street in the typical UK 'Nucleus' hospital (p. 138), introduces a familiar and attractive element for people who have travelled some distance and need to spend time awaiting treatment or seeing sick relatives. Such a concept looks forward to a time when most hospital activity is likely to be on an out-patient/day-patient basis.

The placing of the support zone – catering, stores etc. – immediately below the ward block is questionable from a fire safety point of view.

Planning and design

Standard nursing units of 38 beds are grouped in four-bed, two-bed and one-bed rooms around a central staff base and supporting ancillary rooms. For an acute ward this is a large unit, about 25% more beds than in a standard Nucleus ward.

Patient amenities are lavish by UK standards. They include a large lounge and dining area central to each ward floor.

External walls are rendered concrete blocks on a steel frame. The interior of the arcade is formed by the side walls of the two sections of the clinical zone. Here the walls are fair faced and painted but, despite this austerity, the arcade is a bright and pleasant place.

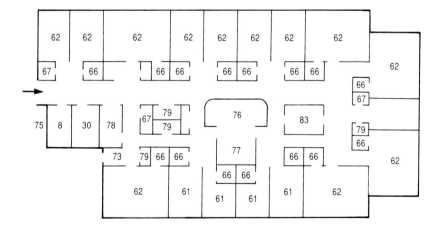

◁ *Plan of typical ward unit*

115

▷ *Merwede General
Hospital. View of arcade
towards main entrance*

Homerton Hospital, Hackney

Architects:	**YRM Architects, London**
Type:	**acute general hospital, 430 beds**
Site:	**flat 14 acre site in urban residential area**
Delivery timescale:	**planning/design 1978–81 construction 1981–86 total period eight years**

Planning and design summary

Development concept
horizontal zones, two storeys

Functional content

Specialties:	general medicine
	general surgical
	obstetrics and special care baby unit
	geriatric assessment
	ITU
Clinical services:	operating theatres
	diagnostic radiology
	laboratory
	rehabilitation
	accident and emergency
	out-patient clinics
	day surgery unit

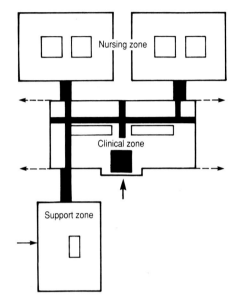

△ *Schematic plan showing relationship of zones*

Homerton Hospital, when fully developed, will become the District General Hospital for Hackney in East London replacing a number of old facilities in the area.

The classic two-storey horizontal development concept provides a group of separate but linked structures each tailored to the requirements of a particular functional zone – nursing, clinical and support. Each zone is free to grow and change without disturbing its neighbour. In this respect it differs from the integrated Nucleus plan (p. 136) in which all medical functions are contained within a standard cruciform 'universal space'. However, the planning of the individual departments is based on the national standard policies and room data used in the Nucleus system.

Winner of the Brick Development Associations Award in 1987, the building is clad in yellow Stamfordstone hand-made bricks which compliment the traditional London-stock brick used in the surrounding streets; roofing slates and hardwood windows complete the domestic appearance of the development. The grounds in and around the buildings are generously landscaped.

In reporting the BDA award the jury commented 'to design a hospital is difficult enough. To make a piece of architecture of it is rare indeed . . .'

The typical ward unit of 28 beds follows that of the Nucleus system. Beds are arranged in four six-bed rooms and four single rooms. A central staff base placed at the apex has a good view of most of the rooms as well as the ward entrance. The L-shaped courtyard plan avoids the unlit internal rooms and corridors of the Nucleus cruciform layout (p. 139).

▷ *First-floor plan*

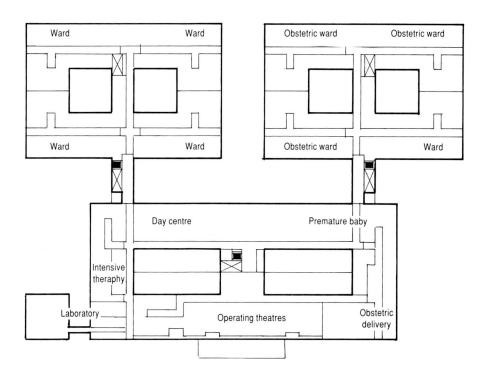

▷ *Ground-floor plan*

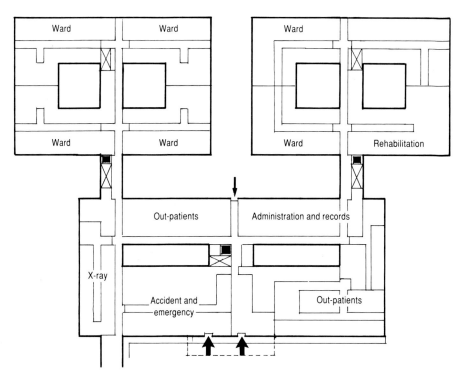

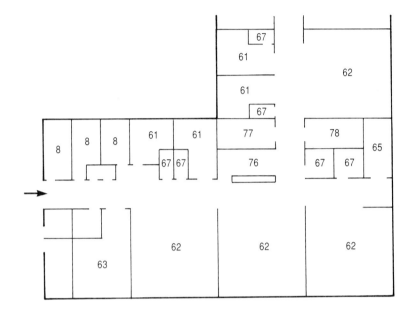

◁ *Typical ward plan*

◁ *Typical four-bed room
from central staff base*

▷ *View of entrance hall.*
Photograph: Martin
Charles

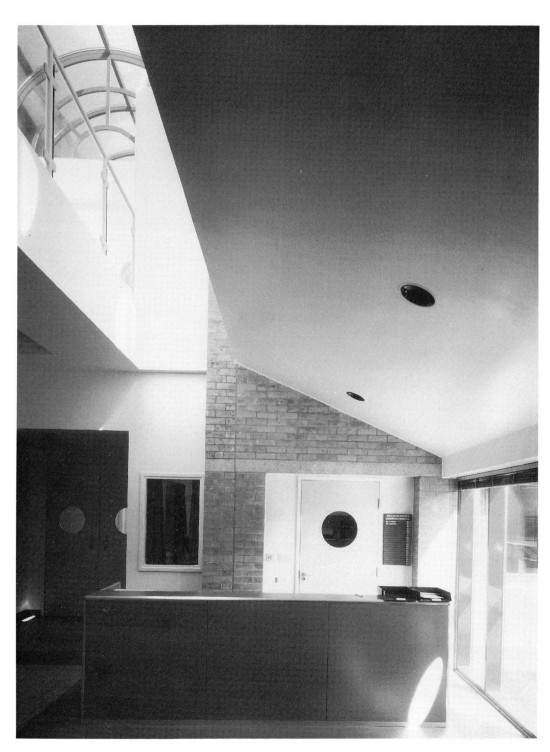

△ *View of ward blocks*

▷ *Operating theatre*

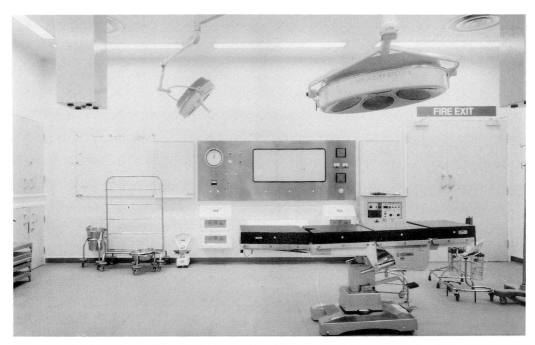

▷ *View towards clinical block showing courtyard between ward blocks*

◁ *Main entrance forecourt*

Conquest Hospital, Hastings, Sussex

Architects:	**Powell Moya and Partners, London**
Type:	**acute general hospital, 368 beds**
Site:	**large area of open farmland, 3.6 km north of Hastings; site slopes generally south from northern boundary – average gradient 1:22**
Delivery timescale:	**planning commenced 1983 construction commenced 1988 completed in 1992**

Planning and design summary

Development concept
horizontal zones – maximum two-storey on four main levels

Functional content

Specialties:	general medicine
	general surgical – 224 beds
	intensive therapy unit
	coronary care unit – 10 beds
	geriatric
	psychiatric – 108 beds
	paediatrics – 20 beds
Clinical services:	accident and emergency
	operating theatres
	diagnostic X-ray
	nuclear medicine
	laboratory
	day surgical unit
	out-patients' clinics
	day hospitals
	rehabilitation

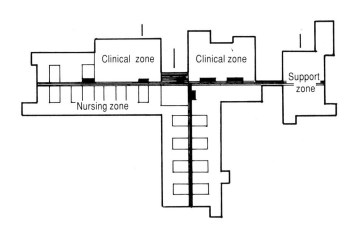

▷ *Schematic plan showing relationship of zones*

△ *View of architect's
model from north.
Photograph: Jeremy
Cockayne*

The building is the first phase of a new hospital of 718 acute beds which will eventually serve the whole of the district population of 156,000 people. It will replace a number of existing small hospitals in the area.

The architects, Powell Moya and Partners (RIBA Gold Medallists in 1975), have been designing hospitals since the early 1950s. The design of the Conquest Hospital, like their pioneering scheme at Slough 1966, is in what is now a well-established tradition of British hospital planning: low rise, horizontally zoned, and planned around a series of landscaped garden courtyards to give plenty of natural light, ventilation and external view. Taking full advantage of the sloping site the architects have reduced the visual impact of a large institution by terracing the buildings down the site and by extensive landscaping including an artificial lake. All four levels have external access at some point.

The two-storey nursing zone is placed on the quiet southern part of the site. The majority of patient rooms have fine views over the lake.

The ward units are L-shaped with a central staff base placed at the apex, to give good supervision of patient rooms, entrance and corridors. On the upper floor roof lights allow daylight into the deep six-bed rooms.

Gently sloping tiled roofs with low overhanging eaves help to tie the building into the hilly landscape reducing its bulk. Horizontal bands of white aluminium 'weatherboarding' alternating with windows suggest the character of Sussex farm buildings. The sloping roofs provide generous space for services and for deep trusses spanning the full width of the buildings.

△ *Main entrance forecourt at level 3*

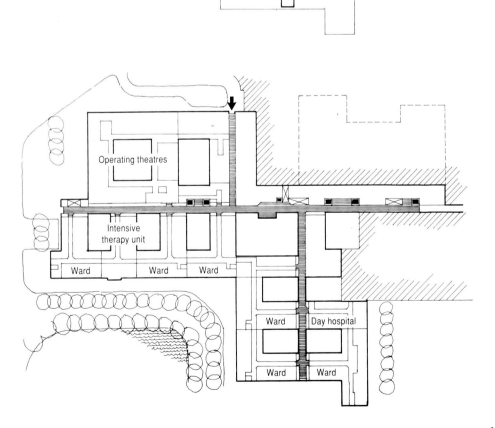

◁ *Plan at level 3*

◁ *Plan at level 2*

▷ *Conquest Hospital.*
Plan of typical ward unit

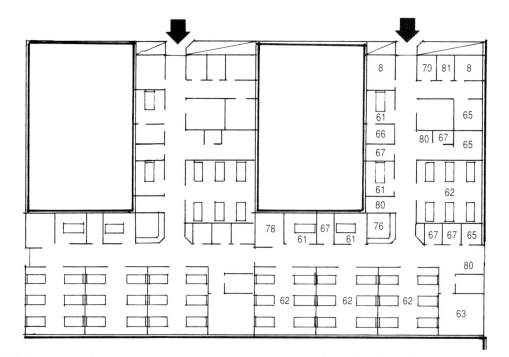

▷▷ *View of ward block*

▽ *View towards main entrance*

128

▷ *Schematic plan showing relationship of zones*

West Dorset Hospital, Dorchester

Architects:	**Percy Thomas Partnership, Architects and Planners**
Type:	**acute general hospital, 150 beds**
Site:	**large sloping site near town centre**
Delivery timescale:	**planning and design 1980–84 construction commenced 1984 completion 1987**

Planning and design summary

Development concept
horizontal zones, maximum three-storeys

Functional content

Specialties:	obstetrics and gynaecology – 86 beds
	special care baby unit – 15 beds
	geriatric assessment – 48 beds
Clinical service:	obstetric delivery suite
	operating theatres
	antenatal clinic
	diagnostic X-ray
	laboratory

West Dorset Hospital, like Conquest Hospital (p. 124ff), is among the few UK projects to be designed in the 1980s, without the aid of the Nucleus system (p. 136). It was planned by a multi-disciplinary project team within the Wessex Regional Health Authority. The design consultants were involved from the outset, as were representatives of local users. By the mid 1980s most RHAs had disbanded their project teams and devolved the tasks of planning hospitals to the District Health Authorities. Lacking the necessary resources, most Districts opted to use the Nucleus system rather than face the delays and frustrations of a 'one-off' approach. Indeed today health authorities are required to justify not opting for Nucleus.

Planned as the first phase of a much larger scheme, the development concept provides for

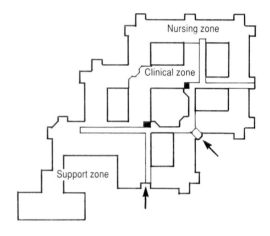

major future extensions of all three functional zones. The plan is imaginative and well conceived. The main entrance – a patient's first contact with the hospital – is particularly successful. Planned at the apex of two identical wings, it has a baroque focality which beckons one in to an attractive space forming two sides of a landscaped courtyard. An open staircase leads up to the in-patient wards on the level above. It is good to see some of the best features of the Victorian hospitals, such as balconies, used again.

The wards are planned around the perimeter of the building. Each unit is in the form of an 'L', with the patient bedrooms (six-bed, four-bed and single) arranged in a cluster around a central staff base. From here observation of most of the rooms as well as the corridors and ward entrance is possible. All the rooms, including staff-rooms, enjoy natural light and ventilation with views of the well landscaped grounds and open courtyards. The design of the ward unit was the subject of research carried out by the RHA, and of discussions with the users.

The hospital was opened by the Prince of Wales in 1988. It was much admired by England's foremost lay architectural critic.

Considerable care was taken in the choice of materials, and in design details, to harmonize with the existing buildings in Dorchester. The predominant building materials are brick and slate. Strong colours are used in small areas such as

△ *General view of*
hospital. Photograph:
Jeremy Cockayne

window frames, doors and external metal work.
There is much use, both externally and internally,
of trelliswork screens.

The external walls are designed to minimize heat
loss. Glazed areas are generally less than 30% of
the external wall but careful location ensures that
there is ample daylight to deep wards.

▷ *(Right) Main entrance.*
Photography: Jeremy
Cockayne

▷ *Plan at level 2*

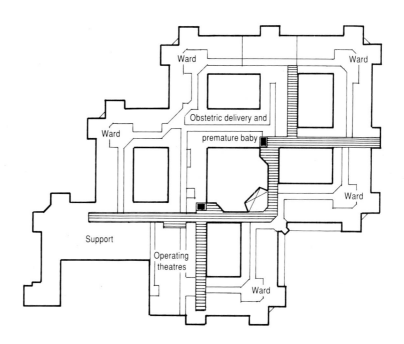

▷ *Plan at level 1*

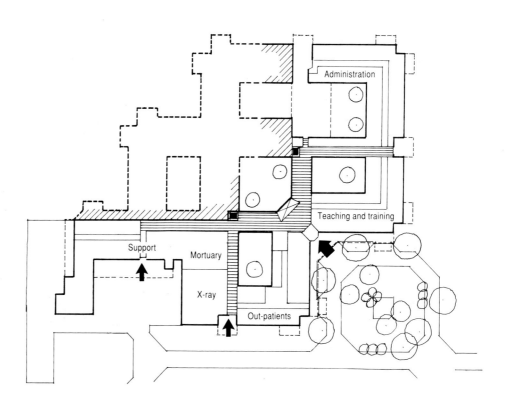

▷▷ *Staircase in main entrance hall. Photograph: Jeremy Cockayne*

▷ *Staff base in typical ward unit. Photograph: Jeremy Cockayne*

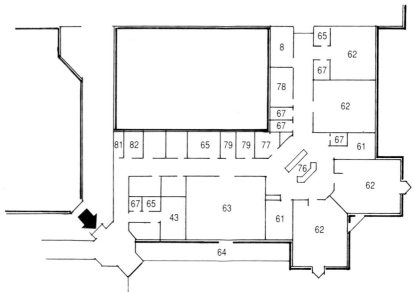

▷ *Typical ward plan*

◁ *View of typical gable end. Photograph: Jeremy Cockayne*

City General Hospital, Stoke-on-Trent

Architects:	**Percy Thomas Partnership, Architects and Planners**
Type:	**acute general hospital, new surgical wing, 350 beds**
Gross floor area:	**21,685 m²**
Area per bed:	**62 m²**
Site:	**part of existing hospital site about 1 mile from town centre**
Delivery timescale:	**planning/design 1982–84 construction 1985–89 total period seven years**

Planning and design summary

Development concept:
universal space – Nucleus; a standardized briefing and planning system developed by the UK Department of Health; maximum three storeys

Functional content

Specialties:	general surgery
	cardio-thoracic surgery
	gynaecology – 280 beds
	paediatric – 60 beds
	intensive therapy – 10 beds
Clinical services:	
	diagnostic radiology
	operating theatres – eight suites
	day surgery unit
	blood bank

▷ *Nucleus standard departments and whole hospital plans*

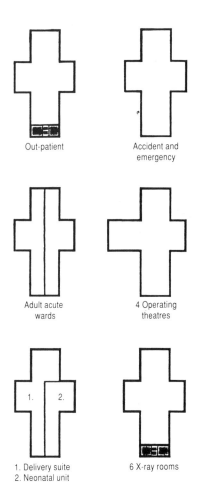

Out-patient

Accident and emergency

Adult acute wards

4 Operating theatres

1. Delivery suite
2. Neonatal unit

6 X-ray rooms

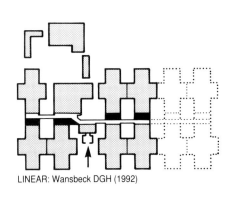

LINEAR: Wansbeck DGH (1992)

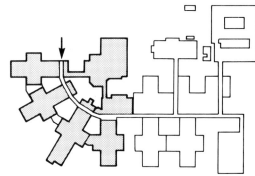

RADIAL: St Mary's DGH, Isle og Wight (1990)

The new surgical wing at Stoke City General Hospital is one of more than 80 Nucleus developments either completed or under construction throughout the UK. Health authorities have found the benefits of using the system irresistible. These include: savings in capital cost, reductions in scarce and expensive planning personnel, savings in fees paid to design consultants and fewer delays in obtaining approvals leading to a reduction in overall delivery timescales.

The Nucleus 'package' contains pre-planned and nationally approved policies, layouts, room data, equipment schedules etc. for all departments normally included in an acute general hospital.

A 16 m (52′5″) wide standard cruciform 'template', with an area of 1000 m² (11,000 ft²), provides a universal space for each department or cluster of departments. All the local project team have to do is to fit the template on to the site, link them together in the correct relationships using a 'communications' system of corridors, lifts, stairs and service ducts and make sure that in doing this, the stringent fire safety code is observed.

Inevitably user reaction, both in terms of functional efficiency and architecture, has been

◁ *General view of two-storey blocks. Photography: Jeremy Cockayne*

137

▷ *Plans*

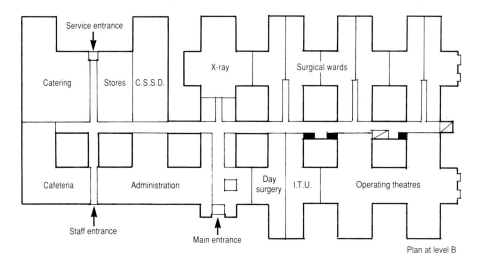

Plan at level B

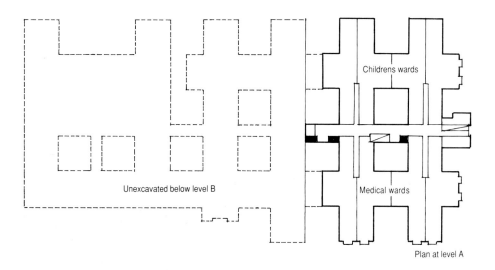

Plan at level A

mixed. A recent study of user opinion in three newly completed Nucleus projects by the Medical Architecture Research Unit found that negative aspects outnumbered positive ones. They concluded that Nucleus 'like the curate's egg, is good in parts'.

The most successful of the standard plans is the 56–bed ward unit. Contained within a single cruciform template, it is compact, economical and strikes a good balance between the patients' need for privacy and the nurses' need for observation. The average distance travelled by the nurse to the patient's bed is 11.5 m.

Where wards are planned on the upper floor, daylight can be introduced into the deep planned areas via roof lights or clerestories.

User criticism, highlighted in the Medical Architecture Research Unit study, included: lack of storage space, inadequate staff accommodation and poor catering facilities. More important was the

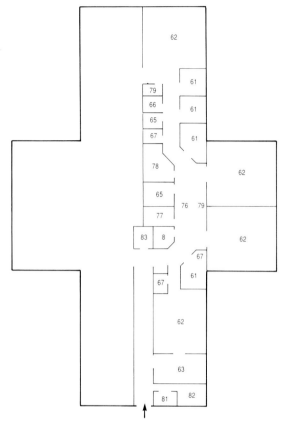

◁ *Nucleus standard ward unit*

◁ *Secondary entrance at lower level A. Photograph: Jeremy Cockayne*

staff reaction to the treatment policy which provides for a central treatment department outside the ward units. Management complained that this demanded more staff and in one hospital treatment is carried out in the wards.

Early fears that the Nucleus system would produce uniform drab hospital buildings throughout the country have largely proved unfounded. At least two recent projects have received design awards. Architects have welcomed their release from the endless debates on medical functions within large project teams. Instead they are able to concentrate on the architecture. At Stoke careful choice of materials, good detailing and superb landscaping, combine to make this an attractive building.

However it is the public spaces outside the departments – long straight corridors lined with repetitive identical courtyards and hidden staircases – which in many Nucleus hospitals compare unfavourably with the Dutch or German examples (pp. 113, 109). It is in these important spaces that the designs seem most constrained by the 'system': compare Stoke Hospital with South Dorset by the same architects (p. 130).

△ *Courtyard at upper level*

▷ *Gable end of one-storey ward block*

▷▷ *Typical landscaped courtyard*
Photography: Jeremy Cockayne

St Mary's Hospital, Newport, Isle of Wight

Architects:	**Ahrends Burton and Koralek (ABK), London**
Type:	**acute general hospital, 191 beds**
Gross floor area:	**17,150 m²**
Area per bed:	**89 m²**
Site:	**part of existing hospital site; approximately 2.2 acres sloping**
Delivery timescale:	**planning/design/development 1981–85 construction 1985–91 total period ten years**

Planning and design summary

Development concept
universal space – Nucleus; a standardized briefing and planning system developed by the UK Department of Health; three storeys with interstitial service floor and roof space

Functional content

Specialties:	general surgical – 56 beds
	orthopaedic – 56 beds
	paediatric – 27 beds
	geriatric assessment – 48 beds
	ITU – 4 beds
Clinical services:	operating theatres – 4 suites
	diagnostic X-ray – 4 rooms
	laboratory
	accident and emergency
	out-patients' clinics

In 1979 Howard Goodman, then Chief Architect of the DHSS, initiated a study on the 'Low Energy Hospital'. The team appointed comprised M & E Engineers and QSs from Building Design Partnership, Ahrends Burton & Koralek as Architects and Giffords as Structural Engineers. In 1981 they produced a wide-ranging report, and were then commissioned to put their findings into practice in a live project. They used a typical 300-

▷ *Bird's-eye view of development showing connection with existing hospital*

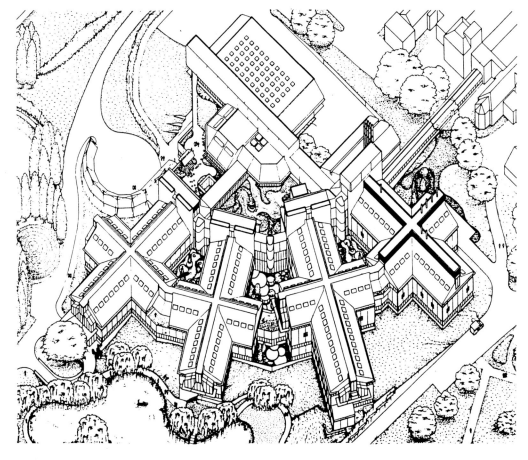

bed Nucleus design as the basis of their study; typical Nucleus buildings have better than average energy performance, but the objective was to halve their energy use.

The chosen exemplar site at Newport includes the following energy saving features: orientation for maximum passive solar gain; location of energy centre close to centre load; cladding which reduces air (and thus heat) leakage; high efficiency electric lighting; maximum natural lighting (notable clerestories to wards); planting to reduce wind cooling; attention to design of kitchens and cooking equipment (which in conventional hospitals accounted for a surprising 20% of energy load).

Many heat recovery techniques are used, and the staff of the hospital have been trained to understand and help to implement the energy saving strategies. Extensive monitoring has been initiated to see whether the expected energy saving of well over 50% is in fact achieved.

The Isle of Wight is an island 32 km by 16 km, 7 km off the south coast of England. It contains popular holiday resorts notable for sailing; its resident population of 112,000 is more than doubled at the height of the summer. Newport, in the centre of the island, is its administrative centre. St Mary's is the District General Hospital supported by several community hospitals. Its site is on high

△ *View from across the lake. Photograph: Terry Grimwood*

143

▷ *Second-floor plan*

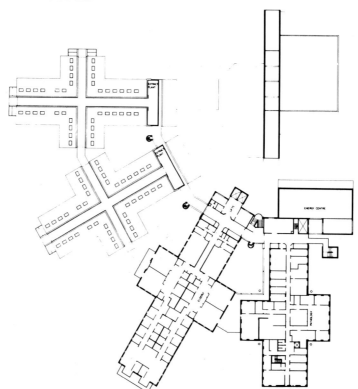

▷ *First-floor plan*

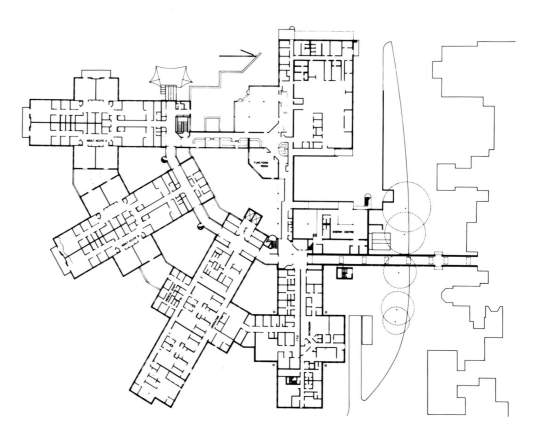

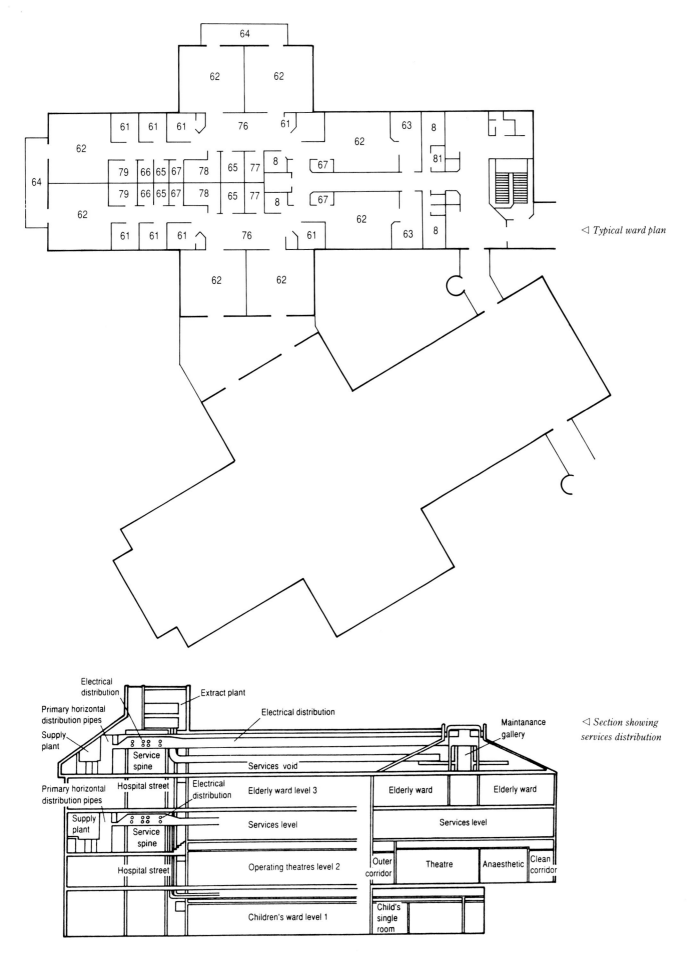

◁ *Typical ward plan*

◁ *Section showing services distribution*

Electrical distribution

Extract plant

Electrical distribution

Primary horizontal distribution pipes

Supply plant

Maintanance gallery

Service spine

Services void

Primary horizontal distribution pipes

Hospital street

Electrical distribution

Elderly ward level 3

Elderly ward

Elderly ward

Supply plant

Service spine

Services level

Services level

Hospital street

Operating theatres level 2

Outer corridor

Theatre

Anaesthetic

Clean corridor

Children's ward level 1

Child's single room

145

ground sloping to the south. The low energy building is linked to the existing Victorian hospital buildings to the north. The only suitable place for the main entrance was to the west. The decision to use Nucleus had already been made. Richard Burton of ABK made the logical but original move of bending the hospital street to a crescent form. This also shortened walking distances (and transmission losses from services) and provided good views and passive solar heating for wards. It significantly broke the orthogonal geometry characteristic of so many hospitals and makes for interesting and surprising vistas as one moves through the building. In spite of its striking but unusual appearance – notably the stainless steel cladding – it has already proved extremely popular with its community. St Mary's has also carried the integration of works of art into its design further than any previous British hospital. This was initiated by Richard Burton and Peter Senior, who have for many years pioneered the involvement not only of professional artists but also of staff and patients in the embellishment of their hospitals. At St Mary's, the performing arts, as well as the visual arts, are being introduced. Guy Eades has been appointed full-time art co-ordinator; funding of works of art has come from industry and from Southern Arts. (Parallel activities have been undertaken by the British Health Care Arts Centre, whose work has included the arts element in a series of Department of Health funded improvements to out-patient and other 'front-line' departments in existing hospitals. Funding has been obtained and artists selected and commissioned.)

Following further research, a second low energy hospital at Wansbeck near the Northumberland coast has been designed by the Powell Moya Partnership, due for completion in 1992. Its site includes a wind generator.

◁ *Conservatory at gable end*

▷ *Typical six-bed ward*

▽ *Link between gables with street beyond*

West Fife Hospital, Scotland

Architects:	**HLM Architects, London**
Type:	**acute general hospital, 390 beds**
	Major extension to existing
	hospital
Site:	**part of existing site; steep slope**
	towards southern boundary
Delivery	**designed 1990**
timescale:	**completed 1993**

Functional content

Specialties:	general surgery
	gynaecology
	obstetrics
	ITU
Clinical services:	accident and emergency
	operating theatres
	obstetric delivery
	diagnostic X-ray
	out-patients' clinic
	laboratory
	rehabilitation
	medical physics

Planning and design summary

▽ View of model showing relationship of zones

Development concept

horizontal zones; three storeys maximum

One of the first 'design and build' projects in the UK Phase 2 of this National Health Service hospital is being carried out by Kier Building with their architects HLM. If completed by the target date (1993) this will be one of the fastest delivery timescales ever achieved. The 'lead-in' period of only six months was made possible by an agreed complete and comprehensive client's brief made available to the contractor on appointment.

The development concept is imaginative and efficient. The nursing zone (including out-patient clinics etc. at the lower level) is placed on the south side with fine views down the hill towards the Firth of Forth. The Y-shaped ward units enable the majority of patient bedrooms to face south. To the north the clinical zone is closely related to the existing support services. A central spine corridor, running at 45°, links the new complex to the existing hospital.

The generous, centrally placed main entrance hall and the corridors bisecting the three large courtyards are well conceived and should prove to be very attractive public spaces.

△ *View towards main entrance*

Small General/Community Hospitals

King Edward Memorial Hospital – Falkland Islands

Lambeth Community Care Centre – UK

London Bridge Hospital – UK

King Edward Memorial Hospital, Stanley,
Falkland Islands

Architects:	**BDP Architects and Engineers, Preston, UK**
Hospital planner:	**Brian Hitchcox, UK Dept. of Health**
Type:	**general hospital and comprehensive health centre, 30 beds**
Site:	**sloping site alongside harbour on west side of Stanley; part of existing hospital which is incorporated into the scheme**
Delivery timescale:	**planning and design 1984–85 construction 1985–87 total period 116 weeks**

Planning and design summary

Development concept
horizontal zones, single storey; courtyards

Planning and content

Specialties:	general medicine
	general surgery
	intensive therapy
	obstetrics
Clinical services:	accident and emergency
	operating theatre
	diagnostic X-ray
	laboratory

The new hospital replaces the original buildings destroyed by fire in 1984. It provides a primary base from which a comprehensive health-care service, to UK standards, can be offered to both the civilian and military population of the islands. In addition it serves the international fishing fleet operating in the South Atlantic.

From the outset there were serious logistical problems: there were few indigenous building materials, everything being brought from the UK some 8000 miles away. Despite this the hospital was planned, designed and constructed in two years. The architects, one of the largest firms in the UK, were able to provide a comprehensive design service including civil and structural

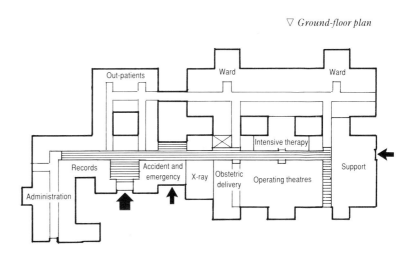

▽ *Ground-floor plan*

△ *View of ward block from*
garden

◁ Aerial view towards Stanley Harbour

engineers, building services engineers and quantity surveyors.

The planning and design stages were completed in 26 weeks with the help of the UK Department of Health's Nucleus data. However the Nucleus cruciform plan shape (template) was simplified to avoid the need for sophisticated environmental services leading to maintenance problems. For similar reasons all the clinical and nursing departments are together on one floor, thereby avoiding dependence on lifts.

The climate in Stanley is officially classified as temperate but in reality it is conditioned by Antarctica and the seemingly endless storms around Cape Horn. The winds blow ceaselessly at an average speed of 20 knots over a bleak, treeless but beautiful landscape. Existing buildings are simple and robust: roofs are invariably corrugated iron painted in bright colours.

For the new hospital the architect chose the modern equivalent: dense concrete blocks for the walls, profiled aluminium roof panels and a prefabricated structural steel frame. As a result the new hospital fits in well with its surroundings.

▷ *Main design elements –*
roof, wall structure

▷ *Control reception area*

Lambeth Community Care Centre, Lambeth

Architects: **Edward Cullinan Architects, London**
Type: **community hospital, 20 beds, 35 day places**
Site: **flat urban site in south London (see plan below)**
Delivery timescale: **planning commenced 1981 opened 1985**

Planning and design summary

Functional content
Specialties: geriatric medicine – 20 beds (GP referrals)
Clinical services: rehabilitation
elderly day centre – 35 places

In the UK the term 'community hospital' was used in the Oxford region in the 1960s to describe a local hospital in a rural area. Many 'cottage hospitals' had

been provided, usually by public subscription, during the previous century, and attended by the local GP; although popular with patients, many had been closed as District General Hospitals (DGHs) had developed. The conditions they provided for surgery and obstetrics were often inadequate in terms of buildings, and the workload was too low either for efficiency or to ensure quality of service.

Lambeth Community Care Centre (CCC) is the first inner-city version of the Oxford type of community hospital – in recognition of the fact that it cannot compete with the DGH – in this case, St Thomas's teaching hospital – for high powered modern medical technology, but that there are many things it can do both better and more economically. It consists of a 20 bed ward above a 35 place day unit.

The ward provides for some medical conditions, some post-operative surgical cases transferred from St Thomas's, respite care for elderly and disabled people, and for terminal care. This provides continuity: patients are near to family and

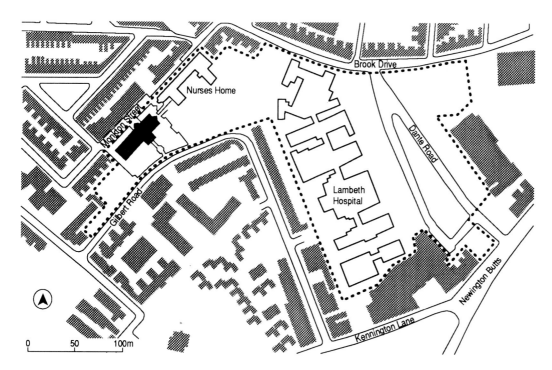

◁ *Site plan. Hatched area shows the Care Centre*

155

▷ *First-floor plan*

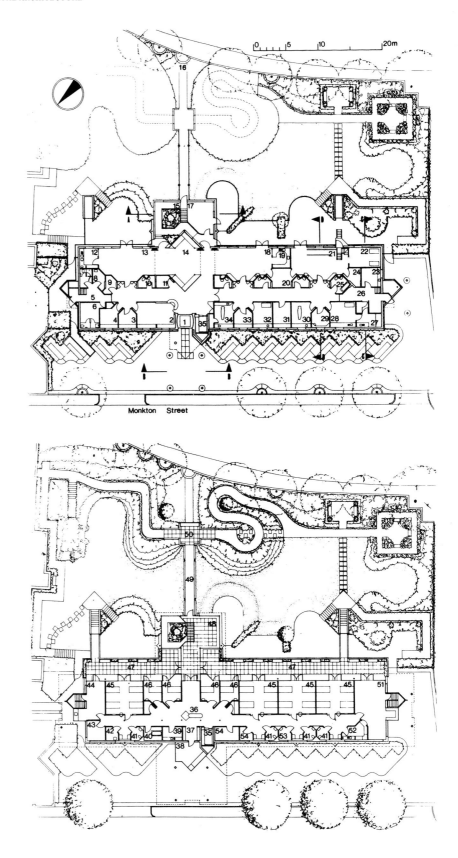

▷ *Ground-floor plan*

friends, in a neighbourhood where many have lived for all their lives. Hospices have revolutionized terminal care, but by the nature of things, they serve a large catchment area; at Lambeth, the hospice approach is applied in the community. The lower floor provides occupational therapy, physiotherapy, chiropody and dentistry.

Lambeth is a rare example of a health building which can be defined as 'community architecture' – the term applied when architects have responded to the needs of under-privileged people, helping and enabling them to improve their own living conditions. The CCC came about because of local pressure, following the closure of Lambeth Hospital. This was focused by the Community Health Council (CHC). (CHCs exist in all Health

△ *View of terrace looking towards conservatory. Photograph: Martin Charles*

157

▷▷ *Lambeth Community Care Centre. View of garden elevation from conservatory. Photograph: Martin Charles*

▷ *Cross sections showing clerestory and terrace*

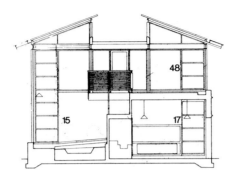

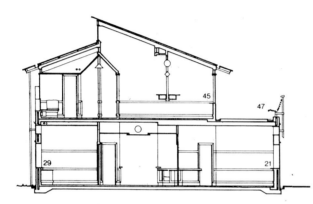

Districts – they were set up in 1974 to represent health service users.) Funding was obtained from the Inner-City Partnership. Cullinans were appointed as architects, and then worked very closely with representatives of users (CHC) as well as of GPs and others who were to work in the CCC. The remarkable way in which users truly shared power in the design process is well documented in a special issue of the *Architects' Journal* of 16 October 1985.

Lambeth belies the cynical view that community architecture never produces buildings of aesthetic quality. Ted Cullinan said 'we want to throw a country house party for sick people'. The domestic analogy is picked up in the London tradition of a façade to the street concealing gardens behind – in this case a garden seen at its best from the terrace into which bedrooms look out and have access. There are many feticitous touches – the stair that winds through a conservatory on the garden side, the avoidance of the usual fluorescent lighting fittings, the downstairs corridor which widens to give passing space, like a country road, and the corridor upstairs with its window seats. To have made hospital corridors things of pleasure is a great achievement; this and many other features make Lambeth a model from which many lessons can be learned and applied to both large and small health buildings.

▷ *Typical patient's bedroom. Photograph: Martin Charles*

London Bridge Hospital, Southwark, London

Architects:	**Llewelyn-Davies Weeks, Architects and Health Service Planners**
Type:	**private acute hospital, 119 beds**
Gross floor area:	**10,000 m²**
Area per bed:	**84 m²**
Site:	**Chamberlains Wharf opposite the City of London; listed warehouse and two existing houses off Tooley Street**
Delivery timescale:	**planning/design/construction 33 months completed 1986**

Planning and design summary

Functional content

Specialties:	general surgery
	general medicine
	cardiology
	cardio-thoracic surgery
	orthopaedics
	ITU
	coronary care
Clinical services:	operating theatres
	diagnostic radiology and imaging
	out-patient clinics
	day surgical unit
	physiotherapy

This is a skilful conversion of a listed Thames warehouse, *c.* 1869, by an internationally known firm of hospital architects and health service planners.

One of the relatively few private hospitals in the UK, London Bridge Hospital forms part of a major development (mainly offices and shops), by the St Martins Property Corporation, covering most of the Thames between London Bridge and Tower Bridge. The need to preserve the deep-plan shape as well as the listed façades of the old warehouse posed the difficult problem of creating the right

▽ *Section through development*

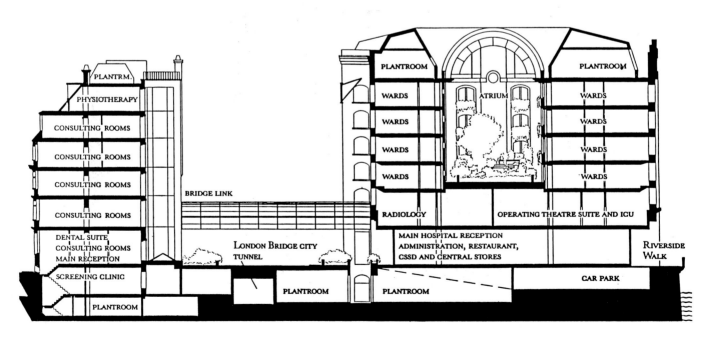

160

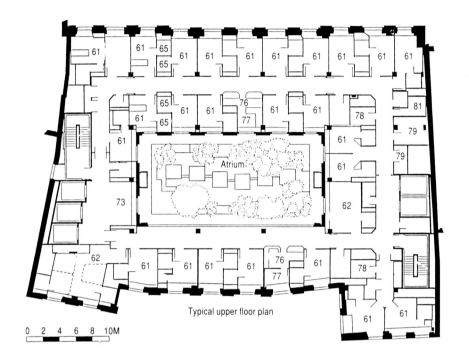

Typical upper floor plan

◁ *Typical upper-floor plan*

0 2 4 6 8 10M

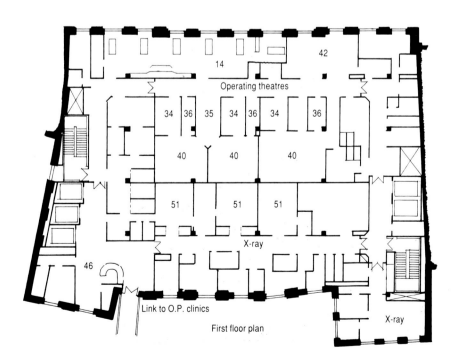

First floor plan

◁ *First-floor plan*

▽ *View of river frontage*
after conversion.
Photograph: Jo Reid and
John Peck

162

△ *Patient's bedroom.*
Photograph: Jo Reid and
John Peck

environment for a luxurious private hospital. The solution is ingenious: a glass roofed courtyard is inserted into the middle of the upper four floors which accommodate the patient bedrooms. In this way all the rooms can have windows, some of which face on to the atrium which is attractively landscaped. The atrium, claimed to be the first in a hospital in Europe, was the subject of close scrutiny by the fire safety authority. Immediately below the atrium, occupying the full depth of the first floor, are the fully air-conditioned diagnostic and treatment facilities which include a special theatre for heart surgery and a cardiac investigation laboratory. A glazed bridge across the vehicle forecourt provides a direct link to the specialist out-patient clinics occupying a converted property in Tooley Street. At ground level are reception, administrative and catering facilities, the latter overlooking a riverside terrace.

Before conversion the old warehouse façades lay damaged and semi-derelict. Now they have been carefully restored. The concrete canopies, lean-tos, and hoists have been removed. Measured facsimiles of the original window frames and glazing bars have been inserted in the restored openings.

The old floors, with 2.1 m ceiling heights, had to be replaced by nine floors with ceiling heights adequate for medical functions. The new floor levels had to be correlated with the old window cills. During demolition two massive internal rings of steel corsetry had to be inserted in order to support the perimeter walls.

As well as providing a first class medical facility the development makes an important contribution to the conservation of the south bank warehouses which give great character to this stretch of the River Thames.

◁ *View of atrium from*
bedroom window

Photography: Jo Reid and
John Peck

▽ *Cafeteria beside river*
terrace

During the preparation of this book, some significant new ideas and developments have occurred that need a brief mention. The coming millennium has led to a number of studies and proposals for the 'hospitals of the 21st century'. Many of these incorporate the terms 'patient-centered care' or 'patient-focused hospitals'. These ideas, originating in the USA, aim to reduce the number of staff interacting with patients during their stay, by multiskilling of staff, for example, nurses who can perform simple X-ray procedures, laboratory tests and physiotherapy treatments. This should, also, reduce patients' journeys around the hospital. A typical model is a large nursing unit, of perhaps 70 beds, equipped with its own diagnostic services. Hospitals could disperse into a campus of specialist units, with a layout like Vrinnevis (p. 76).

Critics of these proposals suggest that efficiency will be lost by fragmentation and duplication of diagnostic functions, the professional bodies have cast doubts on the acceptability of multiskilling. Also, the impression has been given that patient-focused care calls for a virtual redesign of the hospital. However, four London hospitals are going their own way in this direction without radical restructuring of their very different existing buildings.

This approach applied to maternity services has led to the idea of the combined labour, delivery, recovery and post partum [LDRP] room. Now that post-partum stay is generally short, and delivery rooms are designed in a more domestic style, with clinical functions on hand but concealed, it follows that the least disruptive experience for the mother is to remain in the same room throughout her hospital stay, unless a Caesarian delivery or other serious problems occur.

Financial Pressures

In most developed countries, increases in the costs of health care are running ahead of inflation. World recessions have sharpened the concerns of purchasers of health care (whether governments, insurers, or individuals) to obtain better value for money. In USA, the Clinton administration is begining by looking mainly at the problems of health insurance, but the effect is likely to be a reduction in the number of hospitals, and the moving out, or 'unbundling' of as many functions as possible off the hospital site.

It is too early to predict with certainty the effects of Britain's 'NHS reforms' in which the role of health authorities as purchasers has been separated from that of the individual hospitals or 'trusts' as providers. The Tomlinson report on inner London hospitals is pointing to closures and mergers. In other UK cities, estate utilization studies in parallel with service rationalization are defining the roles of individual hospitals more precisely, and reducing specialty duplications between them.

The Tomlinson report particularly commended the services provided by the Lambeth Community Care Centre (p. 155) and suggested that it could be the model for other inner city community hospitals. Further facilities such as small out-patient departments and GP premises, may be added to them.

Day surgery is continuing to increase. As it approaches or exceeds 50% of all surgery, there seems to be a growing case for the linking, where physically possible, of the day surgery unit to the main operating department. This means that as in-patient surgery reduces, the theatres can gradually move to increasing day-patient use. Minimally invasive surgical techniques are developing rapidly, and are leading to further increases in day surgery, as well as to great reductions in length of stay for in-patient procedures like gall-bladder removal.

It is hard to predict the effect of AIDS on hospital services, or of gene therapy, new treatments for cancer, and other scientific advances. There is however no doubt that great increases in the numbers of very old people will make an impact on hospitals as well as on primary care and residential buildings. Already the efficiency of acute medical and surgical services depends on the early moving to rehabilitation care of elderly patients, such as those with fractured neck or femur.

Quality of Environment

In many countries, there is likely to be more work done on upgrading existing hospitals than building new ones. The improvement projects mentioned on page 146 have set an example that is gaining momentum in Britain; these have all included parallel improvements in organization and staff training, especially in attitudes towards patients. Philip Larkin's poem *The Building* (p. 6) can be seen as a critical comment on management and staff attitudes as well as on the fabric of the building. Improvements in these two areas are mutually reinforcing.

There is also growing experience in assessment of the functional suitability of buildings for their present or a future use; in the UK, capital charges are causing hospital managers to get greater throughput out of their buildings, and by creative estate management to reduce unnecessary holdings of buildings and land, as recommended in the 1983 Ceri Davies Report.

The qualities of some of the latest of the new buildings illustrated in this book are now becoming evident. The new building at Guy's (p. 72), instead of the original neo-classical concept, has turned out to be a disappointing piece of routine post-modern; but even so it respects the street pattern better than many urban hospitals. The Chelsea and Westminster (p. 68) is not interesting externally, but its atrium is a remarkable space, quite different from previous examples such as at Edmonton (p. 39) and a striking innovation in hospital design. Hastings has fully lived up to the expectations for it, and the new building at the Hospital for Sick Children, Great Ormond Street, sets very high standards, particularly of imaginative interior design. The success of its fund-faising campaign has permitted a higher quality than usual in the NHS. This is likely to pay for itself in lower maintenance costs and an environment that wears better with passing time.

It is hoped that the buildings included in this book will indicate the scope for achieving 'firmness, commodity and delight', and that these examples may encourage hospitals and their architects to achieve even better things in the future.

Buchanan, P. (1985) Lambeth Community Care Hospital. *The Architects' Journal*, Special Issue, October.

Charles, Prince of Wales (1989) *A Vision of Britain – A Personal View of Architecture*. Doubleday, London.

Clibbon, S. and Sachs, M. (1971) Creating consolidated clinical techniques spaces for an expanding role in health care. *Architectural Record*, February.

Cooper, G. (1990) Dutch courage – Academisch Zieckenhuis Utrecht. *Hospital Development*, October.

Corcoran, M. and Wilson, B. (1989) St Mary's I.O.W. – low energy engineering. *Hospital Development*, June.

Davey, P. (1991) St Mary's Hospital, I.O.W. *The Architectural Review*, February.

Department of Health, UK (1982) *Greenwich District Hospital* (brochure).

Department of Health, UK (1983) *Enquiry into Underused and Surplus Property in the N.H.S.* H.M.S.O., London (The Ceri Davies Report).

Freisen, G. (1975) 'Concepts of Health Planning' *World Hospitals*.

Gilmore, J. (1988) Award winning hospital – West Dorset Hospital. *Hospital Development*, March.

Gowrie, Lord (1990) Architecture and the ruined millionaire – a plea for anarchy. 12th Annual Thomas Cubitt Trust Lecture, London, 26 September 1990.

Hawkes, D. (1982) Energetic nucleus – St Mary's I.O.W. *The Architects' Journal*, October.

Holford, Lord (1950) *Studies for the Reconstruction of St Thomas's Hospital*. Board of Governors, London.

Hutchison, D. (1991) Stepping out – West Fife Hospital. *Hospital Development*, February.

Hyslop, R. (1986) *Nucleus Projects 1975–1986*. H.M.S.O., London.

James, P. (1970) Free movement and the horizontal hospital. *British Hospital Journal and Social Services Review*, March.

James, P. (1974) Materials Handling Systems in Hospitals. *Hospital Engineering*. 28 September.

James, P. and Tatton-Brown, W. (1986) *Hospitals – Design and Development*. Architectural Press, London and Van Nostrand Reinhold, New York.

Kivalo, E., Kotilainen, H. and Leisio, C. (1986) *Health for all in Finland*. National Board of Health, Helsinki.

Larkin, P. (1972) 'The Building' in *High Windows*, Faber & Faber, London.

Mathers and Haldenby (1979) *Interstitial Space in Health Facilities*. Department of Health and Welfare, Ottawa.

Morris, B. (1991) Westminster and Chelsea Hospital. *Hospital Development*, May.

Noakes, A. (1980) Ward design at the cross roads. *Health Service Estate*, January.

Pevsner, N. (1963) *An Outline of European Architecture*, 7th edn. Penguin Books, Harmondsworth.

Pesvsner, N. (1976) *A History of Building Types*. Thames and Hudson, London.

Rawlinson, C. (1988) *Nucleus Hospitals – a comparative evaluation*. Department of Health, London.

Sahl, R. (1986) *Das Krankenhaus Wandlungen in Anlage und Betrieb*. Deutsches Krankenhausinstitut, Dusseldorf.

Scher, P. (1989) Nucleus appraised – the pros and cons. *Hospital Development*, January/February.

Scher, P. (1991) St Mary's I.O.W. – a shining example. *Hospital Development*, October.

Stone, Marraccini, Patterson (1972) Application of the Principles of Systems Integration to the Design of V.A. Hospital Facilities, Washington.

Stone, P. (1976) Hospitals: the heroic years. *The Architects' Journal*, December.

Stone, P. (ed.) (1980) *British Hospitals and Health-Care Buildings*. The Architectural Press, London.

Valins, M. ed. (1992) *Primary Health Care Centres*. Longman, Harlow, Essex.

Weeks, J. (1973) A.D. briefing: hospitals. *Architectural Design*, July.

Zeidler, E. (1974) Healing the Hospital – McMaster Health Sciences Center – its conception and evolution. Toronto.

Index